Why we do
what we do

ESSAYS BY LE MOYNE COLLEGE FACULTY

Cover and interior design by Julie M. Elman.
Author photos by Irene Liu and Dan Roche.

"Beyondness" (Dan Roche) first published in *Passages North*,
passagesnorth.com/2014/01/writers-on-writing-69-dan-roche/.

Publication of this book was made possible by the endowment
of the O'Connell Professorship for the Humanities, and
through the generous support of the offices of Marketing and
Mission & Identity at Le Moyne College.

ISBN-13: 978-0-692-24253-7
ISBN-10: 0692242538

Printed by Eastwood Litho, Inc., Syracuse, N.Y.

Contents

Foreword

Among the sparkling gifts in life, what is more valuable than the discovery of the work that we seem meant to do? I am speaking of the work that, though it may demand arduous training, sacrifice, and constant effort, does not feel so much like work but rather a kind of life-giving labor. The discovery of purpose is no less precious or powerful than a spiritual epiphany, a revelation. Like the authors of these essays, I am someone who seeks to answer a calling of my own. In coming to accept that this was indeed the better expression of my inner freedom and desire to contribute something worthy and worthwhile, I too have discovered the joy that comes from living and working with inner purpose. One's calling becomes a source of direction, meaning, energy, and resilience over the long haul.

While it is very much one's own, a calling is inevitably situated in a community, and is a service to others. The former Superior General of the Society of Jesus, Pedro Arrupe, once wrote:

> Nothing is more practical than finding God, that is, than falling in love in a quite absolute, final way. What you are in love with, what seizes your imagination, will affect everything. It will decide what will get you out of bed in the mornings, what you will do with your evenings, how you spend your weekends, what you read, who you know, what breaks your heart, and what amazes you with joy and gratitude. Fall in love, stay in love, and it will decide everything.

And so it is that love and life-giving labor may in fact be very much connected on this point of purpose, which guides the way we spend the energy we have been given in this life.

This volume collects and offers the reflections of women and men who have answered the call of academic life, learning, and service. While some might describe the academy as the "life of the mind," you will discover here that the work of higher education, especially in the Jesuit, liberal arts tradition, also includes the heart, community, and reflective engagement with students in the world. Each essay, carefully crafted with gemlike compression of meaning and color, offers stories that are both deeply personal and, at the same time, speak to the ways that each of us comes to discover what we love to do, the work we seek to offer in the world—our personal mission, if you will. Whether you are someone searching for that spark that illuminates your life with direction, meaning, and value, or someone who has been living in congruence with your sense of your life's purpose for a long time, we hope you will find here enjoyment, inspiration, and courage in living your mission.

Rev. David McCallum, S.J.
Director of Mission & Identity
Le Moyne College

MAURA BRADY teaches courses in renaissance literature, disability studies, and literature and science. Her essays on John Milton have appeared in various journals and collections, and in 2003 she received the Schachterle Award from the Society for Literature, Science and the Arts for her essay "Galileo in Action: The 'Telescope' in *Paradise Lost.*" She is Associate Professor of English, and from 2011–14 was the O'Connell Chair of the Humanities, a professorship that supports pedagogy and faculty development at Le Moyne.

Introduction

Maura Brady

I n June 2012, seventeen professors from Le Moyne College gathered at Stella Maris Retreat Center in Skaneateles, New York, to write, share our work, and participate in workshops. Although we were eager to immerse ourselves in our writing projects, some of us also felt some trepidation. We all knew from experience that writing was hard work, and we realized that on retreat there would be no escape when things got rough. Yet few of us were accustomed to sharing work-in-progress with others, and the prospect that we might be called upon to present rough work, not polished, to a large group of colleagues gave some of us pause. Furthermore, most of us were used to the independence and solitude that our research, writing, and class preparations generally require, and on retreat we would be sharing close quarters for several days. I was nervous because, as Le Moyne's O'Connell Professor of the Humanities, I had organized this retreat and wanted it to go well. I was also unsure what response to expect to my own work-in-progress, which I had not yet shared with my colleagues.

The weather was hot for June in central New York. A haze hung over the lake that lay at the bottom of a sloping lawn behind the retreat center. In the afternoons we found places to work on our own: a corner desk in one of the libraries, a breezy porch off the back of the house, or a secluded bench out in the garden. If the heat got to be too much, a swim in the chilly lake revived us, and if we needed a break we could usually find someone to chat with over a glass of iced tea. One of us was editing the manuscript of a book scheduled for publication; another was working on a grant application that was due at the end of that week; others had brought drafts of scholarly articles, conference papers, and creative writing in different stages of completion. This was the work of our afternoons.

In the mornings, we gathered for workshops led by Ned Stuckey-French, a professor of English at Florida State University. As the director of FSU's

Publishing and Editing Program, Ned had the expertise to help us think strategically about writing and publication. He is also a very fine writer of creative nonfiction and a scholar of the essay, and I had asked him to spend some time introducing the techniques of this genre in the hopes that they might give us more strategies for communicating with non-specialists about our work.

Our conference room looked out onto the back lawn and at the lake that glinted invitingly through the haze and heat. Inside, the ceiling fans turned as we talked, listened, and wrote. Our first exercise was a one-page query letter to a publisher about a book or article we were writing. We read these aloud, and then Ned asked us to distill their essence into a single paragraph. "You're still looking to convey the significance of your project," he said, "but compressed." There were a few groans around the table, and then the room went quiet except for the scratching of pens and the tapping of keys. It wasn't much of a surprise when, after we had shared these, Ned asked us to boil them down again into a single sentence: the pith and power of our work. As one of us remarked at the time, the process felt like an unmasking, a gradual self-exposure.

On the second morning, Ned gave a brief presentation on the conventions of creative nonfiction, which include techniques associated with fiction writing (e.g., setting a scene, delineating a character), as well as those more common to expository writing, such as summarizing, explicating, or analyzing concepts and information. When there is a narrative in creative nonfiction, it often centers on the speaker's "story of thought" about the experiences or ideas he or she is recounting. At the end of the morning, we were given several writing exercises to try, including this one: "Write a Personal Essay in Order to Explain What We Do and Why We Do It." "Perhaps this afternoon or evening," ran the prompt, "you could recall a scene that led you to write the article or book you're trying to write, or that led you to become the kind of scholar or teacher you have become." We agreed to come back together later in the day to read our work aloud to the group.

Our conference room was very warm that evening, in spite of the ceiling fans and air conditioning. The sun slanted into the wide, west-facing windows, and we were sleepy from the heat, and from dinner. Our colleague Theresa had volunteered to go first, and to read the short essay she had written in response to the "Why We Do" prompt.

"This is about the moment I realized that I had to be a chemist and a teacher of chemistry," she said. She proceeded to hold us rapt with a description of her first encounter with cellular protein interactions: the shock of awe and joy with which she suddenly understood the textbook diagrams and glimpsed a whole new world of implications and insights lying just beyond, and the fervent desire to share this moment with others that gripped her almost simultaneously with the insight. Her vivid evocation of this epiphany brought us wide awake around the table. It ignited our own memories of times when, with wonder and delight, we had witnessed the world suddenly open into something more meaningful and expansive than we had known before, or when, astonished and bewildered, we realized we had stumbled accidentally—and yet inevitably—into what would become our life's work. All of us, I think, saw in Theresa's essay the power and potential of this kind of writing to speak directly to readers, even to electrify them.

Some of the essays in this book were drafted at that first retreat. Others came out of a second retreat held the following year, and still others were drafted by faculty members working independently. Most were revised and polished in the fall of 2013 at a series of after-hours writing workshops at Le Moyne, which David Lloyd, director of Creative Writing, helped organize. Theresa Beaty, Ann Ryan, and David Lloyd facilitated these workshops, reading and responding to multiple drafts of the essays, and running the workshop discussions of them. All of the essays have benefited from the close reading and thoughtful comments of Ned Stuckey-French, facilitator of our first retreat and the editor of this volume. My profound thanks to Ned, Theresa, Ann, and David, for their tireless efforts on behalf of this project, and sage advice on how to proceed with it.

Taken as a whole, these essays give an account of our work as professors: our research, scholarship, and art, as well as our teaching and mentoring of students. (There are no essays here about the important work of governing the college, which we do by serving on committees, but perhaps that is for another volume.) The authors address the implicit question "What is the value of a college education?" from the ground of personal experience, by reflecting on significant moments in their own lives as students and teachers. This is certainly not the only way to approach the question of value, and this book does not pretend to give a complete answer to the question of why we do what we do, or why it matters. To "essay," after all, means to try, to attempt. The literary genre of the essay, as it was practiced (and, arguably, invented) by Michel de Montaigne in the 16th century, was deliberately open-ended, aiming not to give water-tight arguments or certain truths, but rather to meditate on experience, and to show images of a mind at work as it describes a problem or situation, probes its contours, and tests out answers. And since there are likely to be at least as many answers to the question of why a college education matters as there are people in the world, this meditative, open-ended literary art form may well be the genre most fit for the task.

Our contributors teach and work in eleven different departments in the humanities, social sciences, natural sciences and medicine at Le Moyne, and their approaches are as varied as this range of disciplines might suggest. Yet all of the essays speak, in one way or another, to the exhilarating and deeply satisfying work of enlarging a moment of human experience. Whether we do this by researching Native American cultures or the principles of organic chemistry, by creating dynamic and supportive classrooms or reaching out to a single student in need, all of us aim to clear a space from which we can see something that lies beyond our own moment—or deep within it—and share the view with our students and colleagues.

Realizing that we belong to something bigger than ourselves is not unlike the experience of falling in love, and several of the writers here suggest just such a comparison. For Ann Ryan, who fell in love with thinking as an undergraduate at Le Moyne and is now a professor of English literature here, teaching is a way to participate in what Ralph Waldo Emerson once called the "current of universal being," that live circuit of ideas, imagination, and inspiration that connects us to one another. Theresa Beaty describes how her initial insight into cellular protein interactions has continued to resonate in her work, particularly in the classroom, where that first "epiphany moment" ricochets around a room full of students and comes back to her. Similarly, organic chemistry has exerted a "gravitational pull" on Joe Mullins that has proved impossible to ignore; the painstaking work of laboratory research is what holds him in orbit and allows him to draw his students into the circle. Miles Taylor finds the rich history of the English language "thrilling" (*i.e.*, piercing, as with a weapon), and he delights in exploring the ready portals made by its words to other times and places. As a former mechanical engineer turned writer of creative nonfiction, Dan Roche discovers that the key to enlarging the moment lies precisely in those "hard facts" that dominated his work as an engineer, and that it is only by recreating and dwelling in the world of tangibles and immediacies that a writer can make everyday life point beyond itself. And when we see Bob Thurber at work filming Roy, a young prizefighter, tracking him through the camera lens while keeping an eye out for swinging fists and gym equipment, we understand that his disciplined and dexterous mastery of the tools of his trade is precisely what makes possible his deep and empathetic expansion of insight into human experience.

As other essays in this book reveal, it is also listening closely—to our students, to the cultures, texts, and concepts we study, and to the natural world we investigate—that allows us to enlarge the moment. Through listening we can help heal wounds; sometimes these present as physical injuries that mask other traumas, as Mary Springston writes in her essay about working as a physician's assistant in hospitals, clinics, and prisons, and then as a professor at Le Moyne, teaching others to do as she has done. Listening forges the human connections from which healing and renewal can spring, as in the essays of Maria DiTullio and Fred Glennon, who describe their own efforts to help students find meaning in tragic, senseless, or ambiguous experiences, and to move through their pain toward purposeful lives. Scholars can learn to tell new stories by listening to the voices of those who have been silenced. As Holly Rine explains, research is a form of listening that makes way for empathy with those who lived in the past, as well as with those who share our lives in the moment. Moreover, in listening to ourselves and tending to the insights that emerge, we can get better at doing what we do. Wen Ma has learned that paying close attention to his writing process allows him to clarify his own thoughts, and to explore ways of making them clearer and more compelling for his readers. He has used this insight to become not only a productive scholar in the field of education, but also a more effective teacher of writing, one who models for his students the power of revision as a tool for learning.

Often it is our own sense of self that is enlarged when we put it in new and different contexts. Two of our contributors found as students that when they enlarged their experiences of the world, their understanding of themselves also changed. Jeffrey Chin discovered sociology while studying abroad in Hong Kong, and learned the power of social context to shape his sense of self. Orlando Ocampo was brought to question his own unexamined assumptions about himself and his culture when he left his native Argentina to spend a year as a high school exchange student in suburban Connecticut. Both professors work with students at Le Moyne to develop their understanding of the world around them, and of how they fit into it. Studying sociology as an undergraduate not only helped Matthew Loveland understand and critique structures of social power, but also made the world "a beautifully complex place." Now a professor of sociology, he aims to practice the kind of critical and creative thinking he admired in his punk rock heroes. And, in looking back at the path that brought her to take her Ph.D. in ancient Greek philosophy, Irene Liu discovers that remaining aware of her own Chinese cultural "starting points" has allowed her to develop fresh insights into Greek philosophical sensibilities, and, conversely, that studying the Greeks has helped her to understand something about herself, as well.

For my part, reading these essays and talking with my colleagues for nearly two years about why they do what they do has helped bring into focus the purpose and value of my own work. I, too, fell in love with thinking in college. Although I majored in philosophy, it was never ideas or concepts *per se* that spoke to me; it was the *experiences* of knowing, especially the ways that the structures, textures, and sounds of language made meaning palpable. I wrote papers about this as an undergraduate, perplexing my philosophy professors.

In his marginal comments on a paper of mine about figures of speech in Thomas Hobbes' *Leviathan*, one of my professors asked point-blank why I was writing about Hobbes' words instead of his ideas. My problem was that I couldn't get them apart, couldn't sift the ideas free of the words, like gold nuggets from a muddy river. For me, ideas were deeply enmeshed in words, and to get at them I had to steep myself in their language.

However, when I applied to Ph.D. programs in English literature, I did not send a writing sample about words and ideas. Instead, I submitted a paper about the violence visited on characters with intellectual disabilities in novels by Joseph Conrad and Flannery O'Connor. In Conrad's *Secret Agent*, a "feeble-minded" man named Stevie accidentally detonates a bomb given him by an anarchist; in O'Connor's *The Violent Bear It Away*, a boy named Bishop is baptized—and drowned—by a young prophet struggling against his "calling." I found it disturbing that these characters and their disabilities were, as it seemed to me, used as means to literary ends, although I don't think I put it this way at the time. In his comments on my application, which I saw much later, the professor who read my paper had remarked, "She seems almost as concerned with disability as with literature." He sounded puzzled.

I was indeed just as concerned with disability as with literature, and with good reason. I was—and I am—the middle of three sisters, close in age, and our oldest has Down Syndrome. As young children, we were more like triplets than singletons, our mother said: we spent all our days together, roaming the orchards and meadows on our derelict farm in Connecticut; chatting or singing in bed together as we waited for sleep to come at night; sharing one big sickbed when we all caught chicken pox one spring. It has often seemed to me since then that we shared more than experience in those days, something more like an identity, a consciousness, or even a body. During the chicken pox episode, after a day or two in bed, napping, scratching, and watching *Captain Kangaroo* with my sisters on the little black-and-white TV in our parents' bedroom, I recall being visited by the feeling that I was floating free of my body. Looking down at the three sets of legs under the blankets as if from a great distance, I could not tell which ones were mine. To settle the matter, I yelled, "Where are my feet?" and started thrashing them around under the covers. Soon all three of us were laughing and thrashing, and our mother had to come in with her guitar to calm us down. I don't remember what she sang and played for us; we liked "Go Tell Aunt Rhody" and "Clementine," but it might have been "What Shall We Do With the Drunken Sailor," a favorite of hers.

If, as a young adult, I was just as concerned with disability as with literature, it was no wonder. As a child I had been an early and avid reader, but it wasn't until college that I began noticing that the theme of disability was everywhere in western literature, from *Oedipus Rex* to the Bible, and from *King Lear* to Conrad and O'Connor. By the time I entered graduate school in the 1990s, disability studies was an emerging field of academic inquiry into the social, political, and cultural elements of disability, but since there were no courses in it at my university, I did not take my work in this direction.

Instead, I turned to the literature of the 17th century, because the writers of this period were interested in knowledge and experience. The emergence of humanism at the beginning of the renaissance and of scientific experiment at the end had helped focus the attention of philosophers, artists, and poets on epistemology, particularly on the role of experience in knowledge. When in graduate school I rediscovered *Paradise Lost*, I passed over the poem's theology in favor of its captivating depictions of admiration, curiosity, confusion, and insight. I wrote my dissertation on Galileo, the telescope, and experiences of knowing in Milton's poem.

Meanwhile, I also developed an interest in nonfiction literature, particularly the essay. Essays appealed to me because they often took *knowing* (or trying to know) as their subject, and *experience* as their ground. Furthermore, the genre seemed to open up human experience in ways other genres did not. Essays written in the first person gave voice to experiences of disability, illness, and otherness more generally; I took courses in which the readings included essays by Michel de Montaigne, Virginia Woolf, Randolph Bourne, E.B. White, James Baldwin, and Nancy Mairs. Their work struck me as raw, poetic, and direct. I began writing essays myself, and found that this form of writing offered ways to explore things I couldn't otherwise get at in my academic work: my sisters, our intimacy, and why it mattered (and why it didn't) that one of us had a disability. But I wrote a dissertation on Milton's *Paradise Lost*, and got a job teaching renaissance literature, and since I enjoyed this work, too, I stayed with it to write and publish in the run-up to tenure.

I still write about Milton and teach his works. But recently I've also returned to my earlier preoccupation with disability, finding, naturally enough, that the avenue of approach has made a difference. My work on 17th-century literature has taught me that "knowing" is always mediated. The difficult work of grinding optical lenses for his telescopes, for instance, made it clear to Galileo that seeing and understanding was not a simple matter of *looking*, but of skillful craft, discipline, and hard work. The mind doesn't take hold of ideas directly; it uses tools such as language, scientific instruments, laws and social institutions, all of which shape our understanding of the concepts we grasp. I have kept this insight close by in studying intellectual disability. Furthermore, my life's experience has taught me that cultural concepts are not mere abstractions, but lived realities. "Motherhood," for example, is a set of concrete practices and expectations with which I work as best I can. Like any other mother, I embrace some, avoid others, and try to carve out a few new ones, so that my children find it perfectly natural (I hope) to have a mother who is a college professor, who does not usually chaperone field trips, but who does enjoy cooking dinner for her family.

These lessons from other parts of my life have put me in a better position to see that "intellectual disability," "mental retardation," or "feeble-mindedness" are not so much conditions belonging to people as they are concepts made concrete in the world through cultural practices and structures, from residential institutions in the early years of the 20th century, to special education, group homes, and vocational advancement centers at its close. These structures have shaped my relationship with my sister all our lives. And now that our parents are gone and my younger sister and I are responsible for our older sister, I have developed a direct relationship with "disability" itself, a closer acquaintance with the caring professionals who staff our sister's home, the agencies that coordinate her services, and her doctors. I know the laws that determine how we can provide for her financially, and which airlines are best at accommodating people with disabilities. These social supports are all part of what makes it possible for her to live as independently as she does, and it is sobering to think that they have only been developed very recently, within our lifetime.

These days I'm writing essays again, about disability, sisterhood, and identity, some of which I shared at that first writing retreat. I'm also teaching a new course on definitions of intellectual disability in American history. And in the process I'm learning—or perhaps remembering—that my identity has always included my sister. This has not always been easy or comfortable, because we've both encountered some unfortunate and persistent ideas in our culture about people with intellectual disabilities. My sister has been regarded, at various times, as a perpetual child; a sinless angel; an object of curiosity, fear, and embarrassment; a hopeless case; and a burden. Because I've identified with her throughout my life, I've taken these views to my own heart, as she has to hers, not without consequences. Fortunately for us, however, we've also known many people who've recognized her for the remarkable person she is: a woman with supreme poise, good manners, and fortitude; a dry sense of humor, and an eye for a handsome man; a love of 1970's pop music, and an appreciation for good home cooking. She charms my friends and makes plenty of her own, as well. In my writing I try to do justice to who she is, what our relationship is like, and what it means that both of us—for better and for worse—have a relationship with "disability." I also try to keep sight of the main thing, which is this: that although we are individuals, we also share identities;

that my identity is roomy enough to include my sister, as I hope hers has room enough for me; and that human experience is richer, deeper, and more expansive than we often think.

In short, my work, like that of my colleagues, as described in these essays, is a direct engagement with the "real world," not an escape from it. Real life is lived in the day-to-day work that we all must do to pay the rent, but that is not all there is to it. Life is also lived outside the daily routines, in our reflections on experience; in our engagement with other people, places, and times; and in the search for meaning that is an inescapable part of what we do as human beings. It includes wonder and curiosity, deliberation and experiment, logic and argument, imagination and invention, meditation and prayer. The essays in this book not only describe the work of "enlarging the moment" that we do as professors; they perform it, and bring it to life. The very act of reflecting on why we do what we do enlarges the moment, creating a space from which more expansive visions of the world and ourselves become possible. Although these pieces were written for a wide audience within and outside of academia, and are offered in the sincere hope they will speak to this readership, we've also discovered in writing them that we've been speaking to ourselves. How and why one's own life's work makes a difference in the world is a good question for any of us to ask, and to try to answer. There is every chance that it will lead to a renewed sense of purpose, and even inspiration.

THERESA L. BEATY teaches chemistry and biochemistry at Le Moyne College. She enthusiastically introduces physiologically relevant chemistry examples and nonhuman biochemistry scenarios in her classes. A committed coffee-holic, she relaxes by meditating, drinking herbal tea, and doing crossword puzzles. She also enjoys writing letters (by hand, using pen and paper!) to friends and relations.

Why Do I Teach Biochemistry?

Theresa L. Beaty

I experienced a rare moment of perfect clarity when I casually flipped open the book *Molecular Biology of the Cell* by Bruce Alberts, the required text for my undergraduate cell biology course. It was the first day of the fall semester, I was twenty, and I fell immediately in love. The emotions connected to my boyfriend, grandparents, or ice cream did not compare to my visceral reaction to the entrancing diagrams of proteins interacting inside cells. My "boyfriend" occasionally changed persons, my grandparents were far away, and ice cream was transitory, but I knew within seconds of looking at the figures in the book that I had found my future.

Why did those figures resonate so deeply within me? In that moment, I realized that blue and pink circular proteins were in every diagram regardless of whether the figure legend described a bacterium or skin cell. I saw connections between proteins of slightly different colors, light blue and dark blue, and between circular and square proteins. I was struck by the fact that the organization of a few simple cartoon shapes could describe the molecular differences between vastly different organisms. The colorful diagrams demonstrated that the same types of proteins were present and functional in wildly different types of cells. Even more amazing to me was the realization that the protein interaction cascades from one cell could be super-imposed upon a totally different cell, and the layered images would be *coherent*. An enzyme cascade will catalyze a chemical pathway in a bacterium just as well as in a human. The individual physiological characteristics of different organisms are not due to radically different chemicals, but rather to the unique combinations of common classes of molecules and biochemical reactions. For example, the same general types of biochemicals are present in me and in the bacteria that live in my intestinal tract. The huge degree of physiological differences between my bacteria and me are ultimately due to minor chemical variations in our molecular structures and biochemical pathways. The beautifully lucid cartoons in my undergraduate cell biology text book made clear to me that common chemical structures and reactions are the unifying threads between all biological species.

I entered a graduate program in biochemistry and immersed myself in the molecular patterns that describe cellular functions. I enjoyed analyzing how apparently trivial molecular variations could powerfully change the developmental direction of a cell. I spent less time admiring cartoons of protein interactions, and instead developed black-and-white photographs of real molecular interactions that occurred in my laboratory research. Colored cartoons were replaced with "real data." I was becoming an experimental scientist, referring to cartoon models only when I needed to explain my experiments to somebody else.

Which is how I accidentally discovered that I liked to teach. I slowly realized that I was the person in the research group who consistently volunteered to orient a new graduate student to the lab. I helped set up equipment, explained which key steps in the experimental procedures would minimize error, and assisted with the initial data analysis. I drew cartoon diagrams to demonstrate relevant molecular interactions inside of cells. I never noticed that I had (again) delayed my own work.

As I became a senior graduate student and then a postdoctoral research fellow, I discovered that I greatly enjoyed preparing for and presenting at lab meetings and journal clubs. Reading current and historical research papers was engrossing; I was reminded again and again of the modular nature of biochemistry, of how individual chemical steps can variously combine into myriad processes and create an utterly new "whole," a cell engaged in a new activity. I was excited to lead discussions on current research trends in biochemical cell development. After a particularly arduous presentation on a topic relatively far-removed from my own research focus, I overheard some senior faculty members talking about the research paper that I had discussed. They weren't quibbling about my grasp of the concepts or my presentation style; they were debating the merits of the conclusions put forth in the paper I had presented. I realized then that I had successfully enabled an audience of smart and skeptical people to actively engage new material. From that moment on, I knew that I wanted to teach.

The initial excitement that I felt when perusing my undergraduate cell biology textbook has not diminished, though I have now been teaching for many years. My fascination with biochemistry is constantly revitalized as I introduce this field to my students. It is a complex science that is defined by molecular subtleties. For example, if the phrase "you are what you eat" is true, then what explains the undeniable differences between two people who eat precisely the same things? It must be the slightly different biochemical environment found in each person's cells and tissues. Perhaps one person has a highly efficient form of a metabolic enzyme and exercises more regularly. This combination will help increase that person's overall metabolic rate. The slight variations in each person's molecular cocktail will give rise to individual physical characteristics, despite identical eating habits.

A more complicated example of biochemical subtlety is the characteristic of "consciousness." Only a few so-called "higher-order" organisms such as primates are considered to have "consciousness." The nervous tissues of these organisms produce many small molecules that initiate and regulate the biochemical communication between nerve cells. Biochemically speaking, the small molecules bind to particular proteins found on the nerve cells and effectively "tell" the cell that something has happened. These interactions are chemically mundane, utterly uncomplicated. What's interesting is that my nervous system produces the same general molecular cocktail as the nervous system in each of my students, but we individually experience consciousness in a unique way. This can happen only because the biochemistry of each of our brains is unique. My individual chemical "parts" required for consciousness add up to a different "whole" state of self-awareness, compared to each of my students. But how can the same molecules participate in the same series of chemical interactions yet result in such important differences in reality? This is an irresistible paradox!

Another example that is not biochemically subtle but no less a paradox, is the challenge that biochemistry poses to the idea of "higher-order organism." All biological life on Earth shares the same physical and chemical properties of atoms and electrons; that is, their chemistry is the same. However, there is a divergent pattern of increasing molecular complexity between such organisms as bacteria, worms, and humans. Bacteria inhabit the lowest level of this hierarchy and are considered "lower-order organisms." But the characteristic of consciousness, a trait of only some "higher-order organisms," cannot exist without the concomitant biochemical functioning of bacteria. Bacteria synthesize chemicals that self-aware organisms must eat in order to live, such as vitamin B and biologically useful nitrogen. How can I be "higher-order" if my life (and consciousness) is utterly dependent upon nitrogen-fixing bacteria that live in some plant roots?

In addition to its intriguing paradoxes, biochemistry is a practical science. Are my students suffering from acid indigestion? They may have a temporary imbalance in their stomachs' acid/base chemical reactions. Do they have to hike across campus to get to class? Such activity prompts changes to their hemoglobin's oxygen-carrying capacity; hopefully they're regularly eating iron-rich foods so their hemoglobin has enough iron to function properly. Did they stay up too late last night and now can't open their bleary eyes in class? They probably have a temporary neurochemical imbalance, and need another hour or so before their brain will chemically "notice" that it's daytime. Or perhaps they didn't take the time to eat breakfast and their brains, starving for fuel, can't make enough energy molecules to "wake up." They can't wait for the next much-anticipated social event of the semester? Hopefully their bodies will activate certain enzymes in time to effectively metabolize their beverages of choice.

In every class, I have the opportunity to bring my students along with me on a molecular journey of discovery through a cell. When a student suddenly understands how a straightforward chemical reaction can generate diverse physiological results in different cellular contexts, I am encouraged and renewed. Encouraged, because when students "get it," they can't wait to share their sudden insights with others, to the benefit of their peers and themselves. Renewed, because my epiphany moment from decades ago has just ricocheted around the room, even back to me.

Why do I teach biochemistry? I find great joy in sharing my fascination for the molecular functioning of cells. I delight in setting the stage for my students' epiphany moments regarding chemical cascades and cellular development. It is impossible to predict when the "aha moment" will strike, and it never ceases to energize me. Ultimately, I am still inspired by those cleverly simple and provocative protein cartoons with which I fell in love when I was twenty.

JEFFREY CHIN is Professor of Sociology and the recipient of the Matteo Ricci Award for Diversity, as well as the Scholar of the Year and Advisor of the Year awards from Le Moyne College. He was recognized by the American Sociological Association with the Hans O. Mausch Award for Distinguished Contributions to Undergraduate Teaching and the National Academic Advising Association for meritorious advising. He has served as editor of *Teaching Sociology* and is the author of three books and over two dozen scholarly articles and book chapters.

Who am I?
Sociology has answers!

Jeffrey Chin

There's a joke that people who study psychology are looking for answers concerning their personal pathologies. Or that people in marriage and family counseling programs are looking for answers to fix their own troubled relationships. If that's true, then students of sociology are looking for answers to where they fit into the social world.

I was seventeen and had just finished high school. I had been accepted to the colleges on my list, but my dad had been awarded a Fulbright, so our family was off to Hong Kong for the year. I wanted to think I was an adult and could manage on my own, but doing so would have required action and this teenager was simply floating downstream, oblivious to the possibility of what lay ahead. So I boarded a plane with only a vague idea of how I would be spending the next twelve months.

Being the third-generation American-born child of Chinese parents meant that education was paramount. My sisters and I lived a privileged life: white, upper-middle class suburbs, private school. After-school jobs were prohibited because they would cut into study time. But unlike Chinese kids today, we were anomalous. There was only one other Chinese kid in my class (the son of Joyce Chen) and my parents did not make Chinese language classes, or becoming integrated into the Chinese community in Boston's Chinatown, a priority. So I never saw other Chinese faces except during extended-family get-togethers. The message was clear: education (and family, of course) was the only thing that was really important.

As a result, I lived in a social bubble. My friends were white; my teammates were white; my girlfriend was white; my teachers were white; my school curriculum was white; everywhere I looked, the faces were white. I began to think I was white, too, and given the power of social context, I didn't even notice.

Then every once in a while, an event would snap me back to reality. Usually these events involved someone shouting from the window of a passing car:

racial slurs, sometimes sophomoric, sometimes genuinely hurtful. I developed a healthy self-loathing that to this day still resides in the recesses of my mind.

The year in Hong Kong was transformative. For the first time, I was surrounded by Chinese faces. No one yelled "ah-so" from windows of passing cars or pulled on the sides of their eyes. I dated a Chinese girl for the first time. Ironically, my status as an "ABC" (American-born Chinese) subjected me to a new form of prejudice that was not quite as painful as "chinky-chinky chinaman" but every bit as real. Now my status as American was the source of denigration by the Chinese people around me, instead of my Chinese-ness being the target of Americans. It was a sociological lesson (although I didn't know it at the time) on racial stratification. It was also a lesson on the sociology of self.

I spent the year doing what I knew best: going to school. But there were no advisors, no first-year program, and no real advising to speak of, so I fell into a 400-level course called The Sociology of Knowledge in the fall of 1972. One of the books we used was a classic called *The Social Construction of Reality*, by Peter Berger and Thomas Luckmann (1967); the instructor was Geoffrey Guest, a British national. His approach to teaching was "old school" — no active learning, no recognition of what is now a rich literature on teaching and learning. Nope, he stood in front of us, stared at the back wall and talked for an hour or however long the class was. No "Questions? Comments?" No "What do you think about . . .?" Just straight lecture. Talking, really.

But the subject matter was fascinating. The course raised questions like: How do we know what we know? Where do social facts come from? What makes them facts? I didn't know it at the time, but it was an introduction to symbolic interactionism and what would become a life-long interest in sociological social psychology that resulted in my second book (Chin and Jacobson, 2009).

I learned that symbolic interactionism was based on the assumption that reality is socially constructed. In the deviance class that I now teach, we begin with the premise that there is no such thing as a universally deviant act. Social context is what makes it deviant, and social context is the product of social interaction. Without two or more people, there is no interaction, and without interaction, there is no agreement of what is deviant (Becker, 1963). Sort of like the philosophical question about the tree falling in the forest.

I thought, "Huh, that makes sense." All of a sudden, here was context, a framework and theoretical model on which to hang my observations about social living. And the context defined the situation. When I got teased, my mother would say: "Don't pay attention to them." In a way she was right: surround yourself with like-minded individuals and the reality changes because the definition of the situation changes.

I never fully appreciated the experience of being in Hong Kong for a year until much later. Instead, I was eager to get back to the States and when I did, I matriculated at Trinity College. I still had white friends, white teammates, white girlfriends, white teachers, and a white curriculum. But sociology reminded me of the power of social context. I now had tools to understand my world and my self that I did not have before taking those first sociology classes. Remember the clinicians at the beginning of this essay?

I now had answers to questions such as "Who am I?" which introduced me to Kuhn and McPartland's study of the self. Besides giving me the tools to do a sociological study of my self, it also became something I now pass on to students in my classes. Asking the question: "How do others see me?" gave me an understanding of Goffman's concept of impression management. Goffman's "presentation of self" is a cornerstone of sociological social psychology with practical implications for how I appear to my students. I remind them that they, too, can analyze their own presentation of self and benefit from this exercise. Now, I not only had answers to questions like these, but the questions had legitimacy. The still incomplete puzzle was beginning to take shape.

I learned how to refine these musings into researchable questions and testable hypotheses. I collected data and analyzed these data. I produced a senior thesis that is the basis for a presentation that I use today in my own introductory course.

Today I feel that I have a responsibility to pass on the sociological perspective. Of course it is my job as a professor, but it is also my responsibility to do this for my (now adult) daughters, for the kids in my soccer world with whom I come into contact as coach or referee, or for anyone else with whom I might cross paths. That is because sociology taught me something that helped me feel less like an outsider and more like I belong. Don't most young adults feel the same way as they embark on a quest to find out how they fit into the world? I found that sociology helped me on my journey. As a professional sociologist, it is my hope that I can pass it on to my students, too.

References

Becker, Howard. 1963. *The Outsiders*. New York: Free.

Berger, Peter and Thomas Luckmann. 1967. *The Social Construction of Reality*. New York: Anchor.

Chin, Jeffrey and Cardell Jacobson. 2009. *Within the Social World*. Boston: Allyn and Bacon.

Goffman, Erving. 1959. *The Presentation of Self in Everyday Life*. New York: Doubleday.

Kuhn, Manford and Thomas McPartland. 1954. "An Empirical Investigation of Self-Attitudes." *American Sociological Review*. 19:68-76.

MARIA DiTULLIO is an associate professor of Psychology at
Le Moyne College. She graduated in 1984 from George Peabody
College of Vanderbilt University with a doctorate (Ed.D.) in Human
Development Counseling. Maria teaches courses in counseling,
feminist psychology, and grief and loss. As a college professor
and licensed mental health counselor (LMHC), she engages the
power of personal experiences as rich sources of learning and
self-transformation in the classroom.

Professor of Sorrow

Maria DiTullio

I never intended to be a college professor. I came to Le Moyne College in 1994, due more to an accident of opportunity than to any conscious process or sense of calling. I am reminded to "never say never." I now see that what I *never* intended to do was always there—the part of me threaded through the eye of unseen purpose and tied to a place of inner knowing that unfolded over time. Was it fear? Something incubating into possibility that cracked the shell of my hesitations and urged me on my way to the front of the classroom? I was *always* in the process of becoming a teacher guided faithfully forward by an inner compass pointing me to my true north. My soul's autopilot ultimately took me home.

During the first twenty years of my work-life, I practiced in a variety of counseling and human service settings. I loved this work. As a therapist, it has been a privilege to enter into the private worlds of people seeking more fulfilling lives. For many, this means climbing out of the dark and empty well of the past and finding a way to an authentic self, free from rejection, loss, or lack that once lowered the fog and darkened the way forward.

The counseling relationship is a communion of souls in search of our better selves. Initially, we carry inside the stranger—the smoky particles of our being suspended and uncertain. Together, we feel our way hand-over-hand in the dark. Counselors are the guides and creators of safe spaces. However, it is the client who ultimately sees the clearing beyond the gray and steps into the light of his or her *own* sun. This is sacred work, and little did I know that I would come to experience college teaching with the same reverence as I did counseling. When I entered academia, I felt like a stranger in a strange land. There were few people to consult in those early years and I lived in perpetual terror—teaching terror, tenure terror, and terror of being found out by the "real" professors who glided past me in the hallways, seeming self-assured and confident.

Time and perspective have taught me that professors are just regular people. We are *all* always in the process of becoming. Each of us has an assortment of polish and edges. My crisis of identity at the doorway of the academy was not unlike what our first-year students experience when Le Moyne College becomes the stage for their second act. I share with them my own challenges as a new professor, telling them how different and more positive my experience of academia has become. I encourage them to imagine that their trials as first-year students are the harbingers of a hopeful future.

In my therapist role, I was accustomed to a "class" of one, where relationships, emotional content, and discerning self-disclosure are the hallmarks of the counseling process. An entire classroom of students, however eager, made me weak in the knees and entirely self-conscious. What does one do when one feels like a trespasser in foreign territory? I leaned on what I knew best. I translated the givens of good therapy to the classroom and adjusted the black regalia of academia so it fit me more comfortably. I reclaimed the self that I had lost somewhere between my counseling office and Grewen Hall. Increasingly, the priorities and values of my previous career—being egalitarian, conversational, respectful, and connected to students' personal and lived experiences—extended to my classroom.

My teaching and scholarly interests have focused on the psychology of grief. I teach an upper-level seminar on grief where we consider loss due to death, as well as other kinds of grief. My course is both a formal introduction to the study of grief and a venue for students to consider their own grief experiences. Over time, I have come to the realization that students yearn to tell their stories, to begin the tentative search for and discovery of their voices, and to consider their own evolving truths along the way. They are grateful to be afforded the opportunity to talk about themselves as they consider who they are and where they might be heading. I have learned that the writing and sharing of students' stories is healing. In the rubble of their particular grief, students find profound and poignant insights. For years, I have thought that these students' stories are worth telling because they allow an opening to the inner world of their emotional selves. Learning happens in the heart more than in lecture halls. This once uncertain professor is certain of this.

It is no coincidence that I am drawn to the topic of grief and loss: I wear it like the cross I seldom take off. I am only beginning to find the words to tell my own story of loss. After years of teaching about grief, this closeted professor of sorrow has moved incrementally into the deep end of her own grief. I carry the weight of my mother's tattered dreams, made heavier by the generational legacy of the maternal grief she also embodies. My story in many ways is also my mother's story. We are tethered in grief as we were by the slippery cord of promise we once shared. There is healing in the hearing of my own voice speaking the hard truths and scattered gifts of understanding that still connect me to my mother. In a sense, I am where my students are now, and I share parts of this story with my students. There is a grace that wraps around suffering in the telling of one's own truth. It is "risky teaching," but at least for me, this level of intimate exchange is an important source of growth. It helps us find a way around the blind corners of ourselves and perhaps truly see each other for the first time.

In ways I could not have imagined, teaching has become my calling and the classroom another kind of sacred territory. There is a quote in a spiritual text called *A Course in Miracles* that says, "You choose what you want to teach on the basis of what you need to learn." Over the years my classrooms have been filled with young "professors" of sorrow who have taught me that grief is often a quiet stowaway. When allowed an open passage and a voice and form, grief is a mercy to the soul.

Dan is one student who taught me a lasting lesson. Dan's father (a police officer) was shot and killed in the line of duty when Dan was five years old. Since that tragic day, Dan has carried the weight of this loss: he is a gentle giant, sensitive and kind, but a river of frozen anger and sadness underneath. Serious and cautious, Dan wore the badge of injury, but he was also searching for a way past his own wounds to a purposeful life. As the ice of his grief thawed, he began to come to terms with this deep loss, and in meeting his true self, perhaps for the first time, began to envision a meaningful future.

Dan is now a police officer. I was present for his official swearing-in ceremony. I watched this crisply uniformed young man, accompanied by the hauntingly beautiful sound of bagpipes, march in lockstep with his unit to the front of the auditorium. The room was filled with swelled hearts, including my own. When Dan's name was called, he pivoted toward his commanding officer, with posture erect, and his eyes straight ahead, just barely visible under the lowered brim of his cap. The commanding officer approached Dan and pinned badge number 139 on his chest. It was Dan's father's badge, retired for nineteen years. It was a father coming home to his son and a son finally at home with himself—an officer and a gentleman with his father's face, courage, and heart.

I left the building that day under a beautiful blue sky and a thought occurred to me. I never intended to be a college professor because I had not yet learned that a grieving heart is capable of transformation, redemption, and sometimes even resurrection.

FRED GLENNON is Professor and Chair of the Religious Studies Department at Le Moyne College. He teaches courses in religious ethics, moderates Theta Alpha Kappa, the Religious Studies honor society, and has won teaching awards from Le Moyne College (1997) and the American Academy of Religion (2008). He recently authored "Has the End of Faith Come for 21st Century Ethics?" (2013) and co-authored *Introduction to the Study of Religion*, 2nd edition (2012).

The Footprints I Follow

Fred Glennon

When I returned to college after Christmas break my freshman year, I told very few people that my twenty-three-year-old, Irish twin brother had committed suicide on Christmas Eve. My silence wasn't because of shame or guilt; in truth, I don't know what I felt. I just hated the awkwardness that follows when someone finds out about such tragedy. Most stammer about how sorry they are, all the while wishing they had never asked and looking for any opportunity to get away. Even more, I just didn't want to hear people tell me, as they are prone to do at the small Baptist college I attended, that they were praying for me and my family in the hope that God would make everything right again. Inside I would scream, "It'll never be right again, no matter how much you pray!" You can't say that to them, of course, because they mean well. And they wouldn't understand that the God about whom they spoke and to whom they prayed, a God who intervenes in history, who takes away pain and suffering, no longer made sense to me, was no longer a God I could believe in.

One friend, thinking she was doing me a favor, gave me a copy of the poem "Footprints." "Read it," she suggested. "I know it will provide some comfort to you like it did for me when my grandmother died." So, I read it. Instead of feeling better, I got pissed off. The poem is about a person walking on the beach who asks where God was when a tragedy had happened in his life. There was only one set of footprints in the sand at that time. God's reply is that He was carrying the person during those tough times.

"Are you fucking kidding me?" I asked her. "I'm sure losing your grandmother was painful, but can you honestly stand there and tell me that the pain that my family experienced, that my mother felt deep in her heart, when she heard about the police prying my brother's hands off the steering wheel after he shot himself in the face could've been worse?" I went on. "Trust me, we looked for God, but God was nowhere to be found. The tears my mother shed that day tell me that she, not God, bore every bit of the pain that came when she lost her son." I tore up the poem, threw it on the floor, and walked away. My friend called after me, saying she didn't mean to upset me. But the anger and frustration I felt at her, at God, as I recalled the image of my mother sitting in her room crying uncontrollably while holding the picture of her dead child was more than I could bear. I kept walking.

Halfway through the semester, while sitting in my required religion class, the fog surrounding my brother's death began to lift. We were talking about the crucifixion and how in the moments before his death, Jesus cried out, "My God, my God, why have you forsaken me?" The class was small, only twenty-two students. Most were religion majors; it was the largest major on campus. I wasn't surprised to hear many of them echo the belief they'd heard in their churches that this was all a part of God's plan for the salvation of the world. They argued that Jesus didn't feel forsaken; he only said it for the sake of those around him.

My professor looked to see how I was reacting to this discussion. Because of several conversations I'd had with him outside of class, he knew the struggles I was having, the questions I was raising. He also shared with me his own struggles connected with raising a child with special needs. He listened patiently to the class before he spoke, but it was clear to me that he was as uncomfortable as I was with the direction the discussion was taking. With tears forming in his eyes, he asked how anyone could believe that a loving God could demand such torture, such suffering. In words that continue to echo in my mind thirty years later, he said, "Don't you see? The horror Jesus anticipated in the garden of Gethsemane was now a reality. He prayed that God would take the cup from him. But God didn't. Jesus prayed again, but there was no reply. And now the time had come to drink. But where was God? He had lost that sense of presence. He felt alone. He experienced abuse and ridicule throughout his life but God's presence was real. But now, in his hour of need, he was hurting and alone and needed the reassurance of God that everything would turn out all right. But God was absent. He cried out: 'I gave you my all, God. I sacrificed everything. I have been faithful and you have been with me. My God! My God! Why now do you forsake me?' The darkness that engulfed the land overwhelmed him. There were no signs of hope. God didn't respond. He felt alone, utterly forsaken by the God to whom he had committed his life. And in this darkness he died. I believe as Georgia Harkness wrote: 'This was his hell—not merely to suffer, but to suffer and seek in vain for God's sustaining presence.'" Many students in the class looked quizzically at one another; their eyes revealed their discomfort. But no one said anything.

"Where is God when you need God?" he continued as he looked directly at me, echoing the question my mother and I had asked on that fateful Christmas Eve. "In times of suffering, I'm not sure one can ever adequately answer this question. But I do know that simply saying to those whose suffer and who feel abandoned by God, 'God is with you, you just don't know it,' or 'God will get you through this if you just believe and have faith,' doesn't do justice to the sense of abandonment and forsakenness people who suffer experience. We shouldn't trivialize those legitimate moments of 'unbelief' or 'unfaith' that suffering, especially innocent suffering, often brings."

One student worriedly asked, "But we have always believed that God loves us, especially in those moments. Are you saying we are wrong?"

Realizing her concerns were genuine and sensing that others shared her sentiment, he replied, "Not at all. I'm just suggesting that God's love is not demonstrated by protecting us from the pain and tragedy of life, but in helping us to create new possibilities out of such tragedy. Illness, accidents, death are misfortunes that make no distinctions. They happen to all of us at one time or another. Senselessly, perhaps, but they still happen. The good news of the cross and the resurrection of Jesus is not that God protects us from harm's way, but that God suffers with us and will work with us to create new possibilities even out of the most meaningless situations." With that, he wiped his eyes and dismissed class.

Out in the halls, students were talking about what our professor had said. Some were angered by it. "Who does he think he is, telling us that our beliefs are wrong?" Others were confused, not simply by the words but by the emotion he expressed. They had never had seen a professor cry. Was he teaching or preaching? I responded with tears of my own, not because his words made me sad but because he was the first to speak directly to my experience, to what I was feeling and thinking. The tragedy of my brother's death was senseless. We never found out why he did it; we could only surmise. But his suicide brought my family together, really together, for the first time in years. Bobby's death confronted us with the reality of how much we were strangers to one another and how little we knew about each others' lives. His death rekindled our sense of what it meant to be a family and the love we felt for one another, a love that continues to this day. This was the meaning we were creating together. Was God a part of that? I didn't know, but it made more sense about God's role in our lives than anything else.

I was moved most, however, by my professor's passion. He cared deeply for the ideas he taught and even more for the students whose lives he touched. He wasn't afraid to challenge us, to push us beyond the narrow confines of our own perspectives so we might embrace the ambiguity that is so much a part of life. But he did it in ways that invited connection and community—with him, with each other, and with the broader world of ideas and people. We spoke frequently about these things for the rest of the semester and he often provided readings—C.S. Lewis's *A Grief Observed* and Abraham Heschel's essays on "divine pathos"—that helped me to make sense of it all. It was then that I knew what I wanted to do with my life, the path I wanted to follow—to teach, to express the same passion he did for the ideas, for the people who generate them, and for the students who encounter them. Just as he had reached out to me, I wanted to reach out to students who bring their own stories and experiences to the table, often born of confusion and tragedy.

I changed my major from sociology to a double major in religion and psychology. I went to seminary and earned a Master of Divinity with a focus on pastoral care and counseling, a course of study I felt would provide a foundation not simply for teaching but more importantly for providing the understanding, care, and empathy future students might need. I was able to practice and develop these skills in my years as a hospital chaplain and as a community organizer in poor, struggling neighborhoods.

My first teaching jobs while I was completing my Ph.D. in religion and ethics were in county, state, and federal prisons. In many ways the students in those prisons were some of the best I have ever encountered. They had a thirst for knowledge, although often without the preparation most college students bring, and they certainly had their stories—stories of physical and emotional abuse, extreme poverty, and tremendous loss not only of loved ones but of their personal freedom. Eventually I came to Le Moyne, where for over twenty years I have pushed students to take an active role in and responsibility for their learning. I have challenged them to understand and to engage critically the religious and ethical complexities of our increasingly global, religiously pluralistic world, all in the hope that when they leave they will have a stronger sense of themselves as moral agents in a world that desperately needs women and men standing up for what is right and good. At the same time, following in the footsteps of my professor, I have worked tirelessly to create a classroom environment where the students' own perspectives and voices can be articulated and heard, while I offer a listening ear and a gentle sympathetic presence whenever they relate their own stories of confusion, loss, or tragedy.

The beginning of each fall semester and the advent of Christmas will always remind me of my brother and all those who suffer some affliction self-imposed or imposed by society, many of whom continue to sit in my classes year after year—like the father whose nine-year-old daughter died of leukemia, the young man who buried his mother after her long battle with cancer, and the countless young women who continue to struggle with the emotional pain of being raped by male classmates they thought loved them. I hope I will continue to feel the same empathy for them as my professor did for me, and offer to be present with them and provide some comfort. And, when the time is right, I hope I will help them find meaning even in the midst of the senseless, the tragic, and the ambiguous—meaning that often arises only in the context of renewed relationships with family, friends, and faith. To do this is an essential part of my vocation, my calling as a teacher and a person.

IRENE LIU is an associate professor in the Philosophy Department at Le Moyne. She has published articles on Stoic wisdom and Aristotle's views on friendship. She is currently working on developing a theory of humaneness, which draws on Aristotelian ethical naturalism and Confucian ethics. She grew up in Atlanta, Georgia, the daughter of Chinese immigrants.

Being Chinese in Greece

Irene Liu

I don't remember ever deciding to become a scholar of classical philosophy. What could have been the result of a decision was more like the inevitable outcome of pushing a first domino. The first domino was Latin, which I chose as my foreign language in high school. And that choice was more an anti-choice: I chose Latin over French, Spanish, and German because it was the only language I would not have to speak.

But then I became good at Latin, which in turn got me interested in things Roman. And that got me to read Marcus Aurelius' *Meditations*, which I liked so much that my best friend gave me a collection of Plato's dialogues for Christmas. By the end of high school, I was writing philosophical essays in Latin just for myself. By the end of college, I was a philosophy major with four years of ancient Greek, though my philosophical interests were mostly separate from the classical. I liked the Greek language because it was like a puzzle, and because the *Iliad* sounded mesmerizing when Professor Gould read it aloud to us. Given my interest in philosophy, it also seemed like an important language. But I was not especially drawn to Plato or Aristotle then, and it was not really issues in ancient philosophy that moved me. My attraction to philosophy was less cognitive, more visceral—a nameless feeling of beauty akin to the quiet exhilaration of catching sight of the precise moment of sunrise.

It was, I think, this feeling that eventually led me to graduate school, despite having a great life after college. I was living in New York City, working as an art educator by day and hanging out with jazz musicians at night. But nothing in that life made me feel the way philosophy did. Needless to say, I did not return to school to become a "professional," not that I even knew what that label meant back then. I took courses in art and art history simply because I found them interesting. I fell in with the classicists through a seminar on Thucydides and ended up in courses on Euripides, Lucretius, and Plato's stylistic devices. And, of course, I studied philosophy, though I was never able to articulate my academic interests. This feeling that I had did not indicate any particular topic or area of concentration. It was, at one and the same time, too general and too idiosyncratic to be a guide. But I had the languages and a background in classics. So, when it finally came time to specialize, it seemed like the choice had already been made. The foundations were set for me to become a scholar of classical philosophy, and that's what I became.

I've thought about this path several times over the years. There are many, equally good ways to arrive at the same place, but this one seemed more accidental than I would have liked. I am sure that I would have encountered Plato, Aristotle, *et al.* in the course of getting a general education. Given the right teacher, they probably would have been interesting to me. But it was really not Plato or Aristotle that set me on this path. Rather, I came to them because they were on the path I was already on, which began with a silly decision to avoid speaking a foreign language. Given how much I love what I do, it's frightening to think that it all started with something so trivial, though I also always liked that there is in this story a lesson about serendipity and love. Our greatest loves, the ones we cannot imagine life without, could have been otherwise, and that does not make them less.

But that is only part of the story. Midway through graduate school, I read a book called *The Propensity of Things: Toward a History of Efficacy in China.* Written by a French Sinologist named François Jullien, this work seeks to elucidate the Chinese concept of *shi*. Jullien's thesis is that *shi*—roughly translated as "position," "power," or "potential"—expresses a characteristically Chinese way of thinking, a claim that he illustrates by considering examples from ancient Chinese warfare, politics, calligraphy, landscape painting, and literature. According to Jullien, the Chinese see the purest action as non-action, a consequence of identifying and exploiting the potential inherent in situations. An example that stuck with me comes from ancient Chinese military strategy. By taking advantage of the potential contained in position and circumstance, the good general wins before the battle has begun. Winning becomes an inevitable consequence, like nature running its course, and the best general wins without engaging in battle at all. This view is contrasted with the ancient Greek model that is so familiar from the *Iliad*, in which immortal glory, or *kleos*, belongs to the warrior who engages in direct combat on the field for all to see and record blow-by-blow.

Jullien's book was a revelation to me. It is no exaggeration to say that I understood what he was saying in a way I had never understood anything I had read before. Despite (or perhaps, I sometimes wondered, because of) a deeply felt passion, I had always struggled with understanding philosophical views in the analytical way necessary for academic discourse. I felt things, but I did not understand how to continue the discussion. Oftentimes, it was like I did not understand the questions in the first place. I survived by will and luck, finding small corners of interest where I could say something passable, if strange. But nothing came easily. I was told to transfer to comparative literature or art history; I was put on academic probation and given one quarter to improve. I seriously thought that I had some kind of undiagnosed learning disability, an intellectual solipsism, which prevented me from understanding the ideas of others despite reading, rereading, and rereading again. But I did not have this problem reading Jullien's book, though that was not because he is a great writer, which he in fact is.

Rather, I understood Jullien because I already knew what he was trying to say. Despite being born and raised in the United States, I grew up in a Chinese family. Chinese is my first language, and the language of all my home life. I was never taught a Chinese way of thinking; that was simply the thinking that was there to be thought. And now here was a work that described how I already thought and what I already knew, as if it were something novel and strange. The book sounded a lot like my mother. In its light, things she said when I was growing up made a different sense to me. She taught me, for instance, how courage is evident in the stroke of a calligraphy brush, and that the most powerful things are those that people cannot see. As a child, I never realized that other people did not learn these things. But now I heard these things as part of a perspective, which happened to be the perspective in which I was raised. This book was about my starting points, and that is why it made sense to me.

Somewhere Jullien says that he studied ancient China in order to understand ancient Greece. I take this to mean that he studied the Chinese in order to understand his own intellectual heritage, perhaps even to understand himself. In the absence of alternatives, we can't entirely know what we think, and China represented a true alternative for Jullien. In the concept of *shi*, he discovered a way to elucidate the very faintest assumptions about action and agency that frame Western ways of thought. Strange as it sounds, these assumptions are the hardest to see because they are the most obvious. They are also among the most fundamental and, hence, the most important for determining how we live. Thus, Jullien's book on the Chinese concept of *shi* is ultimately about the most basic ideas of Western thought.

This experience of reading Jullien happened as I was on my way to completing my preliminary essay on Aristotle's account of time. It did not change my mind about Greek philosophy, or lead me to pursue the study of Chinese thought. I would eventually go on to write a dissertation that explored the intersection of theology and ethics in Stoic and Epicurean philosophy. And when it came time to get a job, I marketed myself as a scholar of classical philosophy. But something about the experience of reading Jullien stuck, the core of an insight that took many years to process. Perhaps, I thought, my attraction to the Greeks was not as accidental as I thought. Perhaps, like Jullien in reverse, I was studying Greece in order to understand myself. The idea sounded right, though I did not know what to do with it. It was years before I could see my way through to what this insight truly meant for me.

Insights take time to process. We have to appreciate their depth, and that does not happen until we've discovered their sources, explored their furthest edges, and considered their implications. But sometimes there are also obstacles to understanding that stand in the way. What prevented me from seeing my way to this insight was a certain conception of philosophy that can be traced to the Greeks. On this view, philosophy is universal and culturally neutral—in its purest form, it is thought thinking itself. That means that the notion of a specifically Chinese or, for that matter, Greek philosophy makes no sense. There may be things that Chinese people think, or facts about Chinese culture and history. But there is no such thing as Chinese philosophy *per se*. My lived experience of the differences between Chinese thinking and philosophy did not immediately alter my adherence to this ideology. Because they are emotional as well as cognitive, ideologies are the last things to go and the hardest to change.

And so my early years as an assistant professor, the time during which I was supposed to establish myself as a scholar and a teacher, were spent in an odd sort of tension. I struggled to produce scholarship on ancient Greek philosophy, and I did love this work, in an anguished kind of way. But I also never stopped feeling like an outsider. I know that this feeling was partly due to a deeply entrenched disdain for professionalism, and partly due to the rejection, criticism, and insult that befalls almost everyone trying to make her way through the discipline of philosophy. Alienating as they are, such experiences are also the kind of thing one gets over. What I could not get over was rooted in something much older and deeper—the growing sense that my Chinese-ness was at odds with the very practice of philosophy. I began to suspect that I was not just going against the grain, but also going against my grain.

The truth is, I had nothing to say about the burning controversies of ancient philosophy scholarship, nor, more generally speaking, was I ever especially moved by the fundamental problems of philosophy, *e.g.*, the problem of evil, the rationality of virtue, the nature of free will, etc. These concerns felt heavy, obtuse, and flat-footed to me, their significance theoretically intelligible, but emotionally inert. It was not that I had objections to received views, or unanswered questions about basic ideas or arguments. It was simply that I did not fully comprehend *why* the issues mattered or, more accurately, feel *that* they mattered. For that reason, I found it immensely difficult to follow the debates, let alone contribute to them.

I wanted to say something else, something that was impossible to fully articulate until I let go of the ideology of philosophical neutrality. For years, I had been working in and around the theory of ethical naturalism, which, in its roughest outlines, holds that ethics is based on nature. I had tried to approach this view by engaging with ancient Greek philosophers and their modern commentators, though I also always had an uneasy sense that something was off. Perhaps tellingly, for the longest time I was unable to make up my mind whether or not I was sympathetic to this position. It was only once I came to appreciate that nature itself is a Greek concept that what I wanted to say started to come into focus. The philosophical discussion of ethical naturalism— both pro and con—has been shaped by its Greek starting points, which allow for certain conceptual possibilities and preclude others. Once I grasped this thought, I was able to see that my intuitions clashed with some of the starting points of the view rather than with its conclusions. I began to see my obstacles to understanding as an opportunity for a different kind of contribution, and only then could I see how it was possible to do philosophy on my own terms.

"What do you do?" is one of the questions that makes me feel most awkward. I usually say that I work on the tradition of Aristotelian ethical naturalism, but I know that this answer hides an idiosyncratic set of starting points and aims. I am unlike the majority of scholars who work in this field in that I am not interested in Greek philosophy from the inside. Rather, I want to get under and around the edges of its basic concepts—nature, goodness, and human being—by drawing from my Chinese starting points. And I want to do this because I think there are better possibilities for living and being that are not sufficiently accounted for by existing views.

I do this work because I find it beautiful. I have never lost touch with that feeling that I had in college. If anything, it is has grown stronger and clearer as I have gained more control over my philosophical instincts. And I do this work because I have a personal stake in validating the legitimacy of my perspective. I am, like many Chinese-Americans, neither completely foreign nor completely native. The difficulty of this in-between position is not that things get lost in translation, but rather that one fails to realize where sameness ends and differences begin. I hope that my work addresses one such juncture. But most of all, I do this work because I think there is truth in it. I am, in this way, just like all other philosophers. Even if our starting points are different, we are ultimately all trying to get to the same place, or so I have to believe.

MATTHEW T. LOVELAND earned a Ph.D. in sociology and is an associate professor teaching in the departments of Sociology and Political Science at Le Moyne College. His scholarly research is primarily about religion and civic life, but he also writes about political participation and authority more generally. Taking the role of public intellectual seriously, his shares his sociological imagination with non-specialists through his blog and Twitter.

Finding My Sociological Slacks

Matthew T. Loveland

I needed to declare a major. I was quickly approaching the end of my sophomore year at the University of Wisconsin at Whitewater, and I was undeclared. I was more than undeclared; I was uncommitted. I'd go home nearly every weekend, and regularly think about not going back. In retrospect this shouldn't have been a surprise. During high school, I had no particular desire to go to college, and why would I? I'd hated school as long as I could remember. I didn't fit in, I found a lot of it boring, and it kept me from doing the things I liked most: video games and listening to R.E.M. I was good at school, but experienced it as torture.

As I approached my senior year of high school, my mom said, "Go to school or get a job." I chose school because work seemed worse than torture. I unseriously considered Loras College, but I chose the school my two older siblings had attended, for no other reason. I arrived at UW-Whitewater with one clear idea about a major. It was: "Don't major in business."

Never mind that Whitewater was known for its excellent business programs; one of my favorite bands, Possum Dixon, had a song called "Executive Slacks," and that was much more persuasive than promises of jobs and money. The lyric "I'm not trapped in your executive slacks" convinced me I shouldn't major in business. It didn't, however, suggest any other options.

There were no songs that directed me to major in sociology. I made that decision because the six credits I'd already earned toward that degree put me closer than any other options to finishing in four years. Whitewater had a core curriculum, so I'd already taken an anthropology class, and in my ceaseless quest to take every 101 class offered, I'd also taken Intro to Sociology. I liked the content of the anthropology class; learning about cultures and different ways of life was fun as well as fascinating. Plus, it allowed me to say things like, "Your lifestyle isn't for everybody," more confidently than I had previously. Sociology 101 gave me the same kind of content, and, quite frankly, I thought the work was easy. If I'm already on my way, and if this is what sociology is, I thought, then sign me up!

As I took more sociology classes, especially classes in social theory and social change, I realized that what I was doing in class wasn't all that different from what some of my favorite bands were doing in their songs. What I loved about sociology was the abstract thinking that helped me understand structures of social power and criticize the world around me. Songs I'd been relatively mindlessly singing along with since high school were doing the same things. For example Bad Religion, my favorite band at the time, has a song called "Inner Logic" with these lyrics:

> Automatons with business suits swinging black boxes
> sequestering the blueprints of daily life
> contented, free of care, they rejoice in morning ritual
> as they file like drone ant colonies to their office in the sky.

Just like Possum Dixon, they were criticizing the world of business. But this wasn't only a song about the drudgery of corporate work; it was also about the power capitalism and related systems have over the daily lives we all live. Eventually, I came to realize that thinking sociologically made the world a beautifully complex place, and allowed me to say "outrageous" creative things like the artists I admired so much. Sociology also gave me the skills to present evidence supporting those claims. It was equal doses of provocation and verification, and I loved it. Sociology allowed me to be the kind of creative and critical thinker I found in my punk rock heroes. It wasn't that sociology was easy, as I had cynically believed, but rather that it fit the kind of thinking I was already doing and gave me the skills to do it better. In fact, now I see that a lot of people struggle to think about abstract systems, institutions, and culture. A lot of people don't want to criticize the normal; some even think it's dangerous to do so.

I like to think that this basic spirit still drives my daily work, but I regularly confront the expectations of my profession. Graduate school does all it can to professionalize you, to turn aspiring revolutionaries into automatons. You publish, or you perish. You work at a research-focused university, or you have failed. Those who run graduate schools in sociology seem not to have understood the critical perspectives of Marx and Weber very well. They clearly never heard Bad Religion sing, in "Inner Logic," about "graduated mentors" who "stroll in marbled brick porticos . . . where they practice exclusion on the masses every day."

Now, eight years into my career, I am that graduated mentor and, worse,

I've got tenure. I worry about being the "lazy middle-class intellectual" Bad Religion mocks in "21st Century (Digital Boy)." How do I do justice to the critical, anti-authoritarian spirit that lured me to sociology in the first place if now I'm a secure professional spending my days credentialing mostly middle-class kids for jobs that capitalism is busy making obsolete?

My punk rock heroes still scream their answers through my speakers, but now I've got sociology role models too. I regularly remember what one of my undergraduate mentors told me: "Sociology should help people to get along with one another." If careful reflection about how we live together doesn't result in all of us living fuller lives, then it's just "sagacious dialog." Sociologists should be trying to figure out how things like economic systems or religious traditions affect things like personal fulfillment and friendship. They should be doing all they can to share their insights with non-specialists, be they blog readers or general education students. Good sociology, my mentors teach me, can't merely be critical abstraction, because at its core the discipline is about human relationships.

For example, in his classic essay "Culture and Politics," C. Wright Mills wrote about what he called the Fourth Epoch. In the Fourth Epoch, the rise of technological rationality without humanistic reason results in "gentle scientists . . . possessed by an abstracted view that hides from them the humanity of their victims and as well their own humanity." The essay goes on to criticize the unintended harms of the sort of rationality that is part and parcel of the world of work that many of my students want desperately to join. The harms result from choices that aren't sadistic, but "are merely businesslike; they are not emotional at all; they are efficient, rational, technically clean cut. They are inhuman acts because they are impersonal" (Mills 1963, 238).

Mills made an effort to be a public intellectual by writing for popular outlets about the issues of his time. He did sociology for the public, and he did it as a craft. It was a way of life that he hoped would change the world for the better.

When I do sociology, whether it's writing professionally, blogging, or teaching, I try to follow the lead of all these mentors I've written about. My recent scholarly writing has been about friendships, about local activists, and about the mechanics of social power. On my blog, I try to communicate the sociological perspective in plain language and to write about issues that matter outside the boundaries of professional sociology. In the classroom, I work to model thoughtful critique of the social world motivated by a desire to make it better; I try to create a collaborative approach to learning grounded in mutual respect. I do it this way because maybe someone who is where I was twenty years ago, with a penchant for criticizing the world, but without any idea how to make it a productive life's work, will discover the value of sociology.

References

Graffin, Greg. 1994. *Inner Logic*, from *Stranger Than Fiction*. Bad Religion.
Atlantic Records CD 82658-1. CD.

—. 1994. *21st Century (Digital Boy)*, from *Stranger Than Fiction*. Bad Religion.
Atlantic Records CD 82658-1. CD.

Mills, C. Wright. 1963. "Culture and Politics." In *Power, Politics, and People:
The Collected Essays of C. Wright Mills,* edited by Louis Horowitz. Ballantine Books: New York.

Zabrecky, Rob. 1993. *Executive Slacks*, from *Possum Dixon*. Possum Dixon.
Interscope Records CD 92291-2. CD.

WEN MA teaches various literacy, research and TESOL methods courses in the Education Department of Le Moyne College. His research interests include participatory discussions as an instructional tool, learning strategies across the curriculum, English language learners, teacher education, and Asian perspectives on education.

Learning and Teaching Academic Writing

Wen Ma

rue to the saying that "publish or perish" is the reality in academia, writing for me is more a professional necessity than a personal choice. As an educator, I have taught courses that span elementary reading and literacy methods, secondary English and content area methods, ESL methods, English grammar and linguistics, and research methods. In addition to teaching, I engage in research and academic writing. I have been able to share my own experience with students through teaching the Research Methods in Education course, a writing-heavy capstone course for our graduate students. As I reflect upon my journey of learning to write as a non-native speaker of English, I have to admit that writing did not begin "naturally" for me. This is also a point I use to remind my native students: *If I can do it, so can you!*

I still remember the procrastination, frustration, even fear, that I experienced as an international student at the University at Buffalo. In my first year of doctoral study, each time before writing a major paper, I would feel I had too many threads of thought to write about, yet at the same time I would be at a loss about where to begin and what to put down. Since I had to produce something and turn it in before the deadline, I forced myself to jot down whatever scanty ideas occurred to me, regardless of whether or not they were coherent or grammatically correct, or even made sense. As I didn't like it as it was, after a day or two, I sat down and went over what I wrote earlier. Maybe it was the additional reading I did, or maybe it was my new thinking about the topic, but almost magically I began to notice a lack of connection here and there, to spot a couple of errors, or even to think of a few new things to add. There and then I suddenly had clearer ideas about where I wanted to go and what I really meant to say in my paper. As I kept revisiting my draft as work-in-progress, I realized I was reshaping my ideas and re-phrasing my expressions, too. After making the corrections and changes, it was more readable than the previous draft. Afterwards, awakened by that realization, I continued to revise all of my writings more purposefully. Indeed, the more I revised my work, the more my writing improved.

Such a strategy not only helped me cope with the writing assignments in those early years as a student, but it also helped me publish multiple articles and books as a faculty member. Obviously, to write effectively about research requires tremendous effort and discipline for any writer, whether one is native or not. I find more practice does make it a little easier. In comparison, while I have used English as the working language for my teaching at Le Moyne, there are traces of a foreign accent or slips of tongue in my spoken English. However, writing allows me time and space to play with my ideas before articulating them. In addition, my academic background in linguistic studies has informed me of the grammatical and structural aspects of the English language, and that knowledge helps me monitor my own written discourse. Consequently, I am able to express myself more clearly through writing than through speaking. This in turn enables me to project a more substantive professional voice via writing.

As I have become more comfortable with my academic writing, I have tried to experiment with literary devices (especially imagery) to present my findings and interpretations in more interesting ways. For instance, in an article about two contrasting discursive patterns in teacher-facilitated discussion vs. student-led discussions, I used these metaphors:

> Like plunging a boulder in the water, the instructor led the class to dive into the heart of these tasks. During student-led small group discussions, however, the conversational topics changed rather fast, and the exploration often touched upon an issue and then quickly moved onto another one. Like skipping a rock on the water, the discussants dragonflied on the surface of numerous topics. (Ma 2009, 13)

This example shows that it is even possible to compose academic discourse in a colorful style. When writing is done this way, the research report can be more vivid and expressive.

As I continue to practice academic writing and research, I have had opportunities to share my experience in my research methods course. For example, I have used my drafts to illustrate for my students how repeated revisions help to sharpen the shape and form of the final write-up, and my students respond positively to such concrete examples. One of my former graduate students, Joe, reflected on his experience as follows:

I have learned that it is important to allow the idea(s) to fully develop in your mind. You can go back and add to the material you have started with and polish the project to make it shine. This was foreign to me since all through high school and college I would work on the piece I was assigned, proofread it once and then hand it in. This professor points out the importance of really working on something and sculpting it into a piece of work you can be proud of rather than just completing an assignment to get it over. (Heil 2012)

This reveals that Joe was not just learning to write based on academic conventions; he was also learning how to use writing as a tool to practice the disciplinary discourse for his school-based thesis research project. It is rewarding to see how my teaching of writing is being picked up by students like Joe.

In my view, many students are good at writing in a conversational style, yet some of them have difficulty writing formal academic discourse since they tend to write as they talk. For me, the challenge is just the opposite. While I need to retain the professional style of writing, I would also like to develop a more personal voice in the way that my students do. In particular, I aspire to acquiring more skills for doing semi-formal writing—a style that is not as rigid as in a formal textbook, but as interactive as an engaging conversation. I think the pervasive social media gives rise to more and more new genres and new practices of writing. The new media and new genres will require us to consider how to change the voice and style of writing in order to fit the occasion and to reach different audiences. So, my goal for the next phase of my journey in learning and teaching academic writing is to learn to write in a more inviting way.

References

Heil, Joseph. Nov. 26, 2012. Research Journal. Le Moyne College. (Quoted with permission)

Ma, Wen. 2009. "Diving into an issue and dragonflying on the surface: Two contrastive discourse patterns of class discussions." *Mid-Western Educational Researcher* 22:7-15.

JOSEPH J. MULLINS, originally from North Tonawanda, New York, graduated from the Rochester Institute of Technology (B.S. Chemistry, 1990) and from the University of Rochester (Ph.D. Chemistry, 1996). He has held professorships at Salisbury State University, Maryland, and the Rochester Institute of Technology. Since 1999 he has been at Le Moyne College, where he is now an associate professor in the Department of Chemistry & Physics.

The Light of the Guiding Moon

Joseph J. Mullins

I knew from an early age that I loved science. I had a remedial chemistry set as a child and loved to see the physical changes that arose from chemical changes. Even now, I look for changes in my students that result from the study of chemistry. I devoured popular scientific texts, explored the library and relished learning—things that I still enjoy. I found that the library was not a closed room but a selection of portals to other places, times, and states of mind. I was the kid who was told by his peers that he would be a scientist because I froze insects in water and tried to revive them. (It never worked.) I also studied with interest the details of a grasshopper under a magnifying glass, and noted the ramifications of concentrated sunlight on their alien-like features—frenzied action followed by stillness and darkening among irregular smoky spirals.

My Christmas list often included items like a telescope, which I did receive (I am indebted to my parents for such indulgences), and which I used on many evenings to study the bright surface of the moon. In the cool, dark stillness of night I was absorbed in a search for the finer features of the universe, but they remained hidden, either by the limitations of my equipment, or by my lack of understanding of how the rotation of the earth can confound maintaining focus on a small heavenly body. A star or planet would exit my optics unrecognized like a passing stranger. It is said that when the moon is out you cannot run fast enough to get away from it. The same has been true of science in my life: even when it is obscured by the clouds of distraction, or in a new phase darkened from obvious view, it has remained in my life, sometimes below the horizon but always exerting its unseen gravitational pull. I had now found a life of inquiry, brought to clarity beneath its illuminating rays. Like many in my time and place in culture, and certainly in society today, I was distracted by sports and the other normal (and mostly healthy) preoccupations of youth. I inadequately utilized the adequate education that I was offered. Little in my limited academic sphere encouraged, let alone mandated, focus or excellence, yet the thought of resuming my passion always returned, and I was comforted by the Lao-tzu aphorism that "the journey of a thousand miles begins with a single footstep." When I let go of unworthy things and drifted without a guide, the natural force would tug at me. Deep down, like the earth, my interior swirled like molten iron, and like the earth without its moon, I would spin irregularly without the stabilizing effect of learning and knowledge. This for me reached its epitome at places of higher education. I knew that I loved the environment of a college; even in my pointless years I would bicycle past a junior college and be gripped in semi-religious wonder and curiosity. This was where learning occurred, where first footsteps were taken and where the mind trained to gain stamina and run. Here was a nexus of growth and purpose and discovery. I took to my community college with a hunger for achievement to make up for lost opportunities.

To learn, share, and encourage discovery became my goal. When I was a teaching assistant in graduate school, a student came to my office hours for help and advice on a very challenging problem. The student subsequently did well on that type of problem on the test and reported to the professor that I was instrumental in her success. That feedback made me realize that I could make a positive difference—another planet was helped into a stable orbit. This purpose filled me; stubborn reagents were uncaring of my efforts and mute in reply to many weeks of experimental entreaties. It is known in quantum physics that the act of observing subatomic particles can alter their behavior. So it is with education: to share with students an exploration of the physical is to change the process positively.

Such is research mentoring, exploring some unknown recess, finding a gem and sharing in the discovery.

Passion and enjoyment can come when realization of one's power of discernment is sharpened. My journey from a student to grad student to teacher led me to publish the article "Six Pillars of Organic Chemistry." This outline of concepts can help explain the various and seemingly unconnected observations of the science of organic chemistry. I am careful to realize, however, that while what I do has purpose and a reason, I alone cannot cure the misled mind or straighten the full-grown tree. I know why I do what I do but realize that not all of my goals will be achieved. I recall the story of the Ph.D. who was introduced to his family as "doctor-so-and-so." When asked by a young nephew if he could heal him when he got sick, a bystander replied, "No, he is the type of doctor who can't help anyone." My students have loved this story, either for its truth, its irony, or some other reason I cannot discern.

As a scientist my tendency to think in broad terms and to make overarching connections must be balanced by the painstaking preparation and detail that comprises so much of laboratory research. Yet both of these aspects can coexist and thrive beneath a benevolent light that brightens my way. I do what I do because I regained my path and I will follow it to my destiny, which is fulfilled with each day. To succeed one must persist and be aware of such guidance. Then can one enjoy the journey, reflect on successes, and enjoy that ineffable silent satisfaction of time well spent.

ORLANDO OCAMPO is an associate professor of Spanish at
Le Moyne. He teaches courses in Spanish language and
Latin American literature. He has been part of the Honors
course in Guatemala since its inception. He has directed study
abroad courses in the Dominican Republic, and led service-
learning trips to Mexico, Dominica, and, most recently, Ecuador.
He sells a piece of his soul every time the college offers him
the chance to travel abroad.

Studying Abroad

Orlando Ocampo

I n 2008, during a ceremony for Maximón, in Zunil, twenty kilometers north of Quetzaltenango, in Guatemala, a shy female student in our study-abroad group passed out in the cramped space designated as the god's sanctuary. She fell like a broken reed on the densely packed dirt floor of the house, overwhelmed either by the dense smoke of the colored candles offered by the faithful in prayer, or the smell from the heavily seasoned chicken and corn stew being prepared for the pilgrims in the back room. Perhaps what had actually triggered her faint had been the sight, the sounds, and the feel of poverty in the claustrophobic back alleys of the surrounding neighborhood, covered from the harsh light and heat of the sun by sheets of blue plastic tarp. Her boyfriend, a husky twenty-one-year-old business major, yelled frantically at the top of his voice, "What the hell are we *doing* here?" while pacing in the courtyard, oblivious to the efforts of the Maya women to revive and comfort his girlfriend. With the patience and equanimity that old age can sometimes bring and with the authority of our charge, my colleague and I managed to assuage his fears for her safety and remind him of the purpose of the class, but his—and her—reluctance to even understand what they had seen carried on for the duration of the trip, and they ended up hating the whole experience. That evening, I couldn't help wondering how many in that group were asking themselves and each other the same question about why they had come there.

Since 1995, I have been involved with study abroad in one way or another: directing courses that last between two weeks and four months, taking part in service-learning experiences to Latin America and the Caribbean, or simply advising students to expand their intellectual and affective horizons by studying abroad. As chair of my department, I also gained the support of my colleagues for instituting a study-abroad requirement for our majors. Students want to go abroad for many reasons, some to advance their careers, many to do tourism, and all of them to have as much fun—whatever that means—as possible. Most of their parents, on the other hand, want them to learn to "appreciate what they have at home." I actually do not disagree with any of those reasons, all equally valid, but my reason for encouraging and supporting study abroad is for the potential transformative effect the experience may have on young peoples' lives.

The course in Guatemala takes between fourteen and eighteen students from Le Moyne College for a three- to four-week interdisciplinary experience designed for the Honors Program by my colleague Mario Sáenz from the Philosophy Department to challenge the average American student's Eurocentric perception from the perspective of the Other. It attracts students from different majors, most of whom have never been outside the United States and find this faculty-led experience sufficiently safe to venture on. Some students never get past the lack of amenities, such as permanent hot water and access to technology, and they tend to stay on the surface of the whole experience. However, many of them do rise to the challenge of overcoming discomfort and the unfamiliar surroundings, and they immerse themselves, albeit for a short while, in the daily life of the host culture and discover revelatory moments that put into question some of the long-held and cherished stereotypes they grew up with. Once, after a long night of coffee and beer, a senior majoring in business and a card-carrying Republican history student, both extremely critical of what they were calling Obama's "socialism," were able to suspend facile platitudes and join me in a complex and difficult discussion that considered alternatives to business as usual. A comment by a guest speaker at the local Jesuit university, on the problems affecting countries with a dependent economy like Guatemala and most of the world, had triggered, after the initial knee-jerk reaction, enough intellectual curiosity to lead them to a serious reflection on the value of a strong government actively engaged in working for the well-being of the majority of the population—a notion, until then, alien, and even dangerous, to them.

I was seventeen years old when I studied abroad for the first time. My father had always thought that my education would be incomplete without studying abroad and, perhaps desiring to live vicariously through his son, encouraged me to apply. So, in 1966, I traveled to Norwalk, Conn., as an American Field Service exchange student to live with a family and attend high school for one year. Besides the obvious practical benefit of becoming fluent in English, my reasons for coming were the possibility of visiting places formerly only imagined, or glimpsed in black-and-white, through books and films, and, naturally, the chance to make the acquaintance of some American girls. In short, I had come to learn something about American culture and to enjoy what, in fact, amounted to a long vacation, since my academic performance at the American high school would not have any effect on my GPA back home. What I had not counted on was how that first time abroad would inexorably, but without me knowing, lead me through a process of taking a serious look at myself, at my own country, and at my own culture from a radically different perspective.

Coming from a country such as Argentina, with a strong European influence, not unlike that of the U.S., I never expected to have difficulty adjusting to life here. Moreover, the advantages in comfort—central heating and air conditioning, and, more importantly, the novelty of color television—held lots of promises, but it did not take very long for me to start having serious second thoughts about my decision. The new life forced me, among other things, to share, for the first time, space with three other siblings, two of whom were girls, a truly unexpectedly taxing experience. Moreover, I even had to give up the privileges of my spoiled-brat upbringing—I was expected to make my own bed, for God's sake! I also had to constrain my social life to after-school programs and limited public spaces, such as the McDonald's on Main Street, where, by the way, given the strict rules of the program, I could not go unless somebody else drove me. So, on the fourth night of my new life, looking out the small window from the half of the old attic that would house me for eleven months and sixteen days, the enormity of the change finally hit me, and I cursed myself for leaving behind my graduating class, a busy café life, my rugby team, now firmly on its way to a sure championship, and the serious possibility of finally hooking up with Teresita Signorelli, the captain of the field hockey team.

The Keatings, my host family, were warm, welcoming, and understanding of my bumbling efforts to fit in. My American mom, in particular, would patiently listen to my complaints and ceaselessly explain the how—and the why—of the new norms. She was not always successful in her efforts, however, and we would sometimes get stuck at the barrier of linguistic and cultural understanding, unable to cross it, like the time she insisted on using the adjective *nice* to describe girls whose physical likeness I was trying to piece together, until it dawned on me that the gorgeous red-head I actually wanted to ask out to the Homecoming Dance perhaps did not fit her definition of nice. It took her and the rest of the family and friends two to three months to get me to stop complaining about the new customs and begin not only to understand the new ways but even to accept some of them. Building my social life around soccer games and track meets was not so bad, after all, because there were always the long bus rides with cheerleaders whose smiles never failed to enhance a victory or soothe a loss—where have you gone, Cathy Marron, our Homecoming Queen? The team turns its lonely eyes to you, woo, woo, woo.

The deeper, long-lasting changes took much longer. In fact, most of them only got their start during that first year but did not bear fruit until later. I did learn a lot about the new country, some as the result of classes on U.S. history and literature I had to take. The rest, the most important part, was the result of probing questions that would surface now and again in conversation, either with Americans, young and older, who would infuriate me with their candid inquiries as to whether there were Indians in Argentina. (There were, but, in my sheltered city-boy life, I didn't know it then.) Other times, the learning came in talks with representatives of the countries that made AFS truly international, like the time Johan, from Austria, asked me whether I considered myself a Democrat or a Republican, an occasion that after mumbling some inane response, sent me running to research the difference between the two. Or, when Negussu Tamrat, from Addis Ababa, wanted to know my opinion about Juan Carlos Onganía, the Army general who had led the latest coup in Argentina, as we unpacked in the room we would share in a visit to Greenwich. Until then, I had prized myself for being a widely read, better-informed-than-the-average-Argentine kind of guy, but moments such as those humbled me for my lack of knowledge, most importantly, because they required me to do some soul searching I had never had to do before. When the time came to head back home, I was a changed person, definitely more critical of the dogmas and the prejudices I had grown up with. Without that first trip, I doubt I would ever have had the courage to venture outside the physical and spiritual comfort of my hometown, and most certainly I wouldn't have traveled as much as I have.

I am convinced that spending time abroad, in close contact with as many diverse people as possible, has cured me of my provincialism and helped strip bare the unexamined exceptionalism my own country claimed for itself. Thus, in 2002, when my friend Mario invited me to join him on the Guatemala trip, I jumped at the chance. It takes a lot of planning and a lot of patience to run such a trip. In every one, there is always at least one student who curses the time he or she decided to come along and questions the value of studying abroad. Every time, the comments chip away at my pedagogical commitment to the power of the experience, but I always remember my own growing pains and hope that, like me, the student will eventually also get past his or her complaints and learn something about the world and the self.

HOLLY RINE is Associate Professor of History at Le Moyne and teaches courses in colonial American, revolutionary American, Native American and world history. Her publications to date have concerned Euro-Indian relations in 17th-century Northeast North America. Along with taking on new research topics dealing with animals in early American history, she can be found walking around campus talking through her most recent research and writing dilemma with Shelby the Wonder Dog.

Other Voices Heard From

Holly Rine

"**I** am going to write the history of the pig in Colonial America," I jokingly told my dissertation advisor. We were in one of our regular progress meetings, but I wasn't making a heck of a lot of progress on my dissertation at that point. I was, however, finding out all sorts of interesting information about pigs in my research. Research that was not supposed to be about pigs. So after I reported on my progress, which was that I found all this cool stuff about pigs, my advisor gave me a look that didn't need to be accompanied by words, but she spoke anyway and she made it clear she was not joking: "Finish your dissertation first." It seems the punch line of that joke I thought I was telling over ten years ago is that, nine years after finishing that dissertation, I am researching and writing about pigs as well as horses and rats and dogs; I'm particularly interested in dogs, but more on that later.

I didn't become an historian to write about animals. I became an historian to study colonial America. I was drawn to the study of history mostly because I was, and still am, fascinated by why people act in certain ways and make particular choices. I was particularly interested in colonial America because in those earliest encounters, it seemed that history could have played out very differently than it did. People of African descent were not automatically thought of as slaves. England did not appear to be poised to launch an empire. Indians were crucial and powerful players in those first cross-cultural contact experiences. I was particularly interested in Indians. Indians had always fascinated me, starting with a romantic interest in them as a bitter kindergartner who was forced to dress as a Pilgrim for the class Thanksgiving celebration instead of being chosen to be an Indian, a crushing blow for four-year-old me. Seventh grade brought New York State history and stories of Iroquois slow-roasting Jesuits alive. This experience also served as justification for my bitterness of seven years earlier: the religious folks just didn't meet a good end. Eventually, as I matured, so did my understanding of Indians and Indian history, which is a history that is difficult to uncover. The written historical record allows historians to learn what Europeans in the past thought about Indians, but not necessarily what the Indians thought about others or themselves. Jesuits describing the ritualistic torture and cannibalization of their colleagues did not provide a fair and balanced account. However, theirs is the written account that exists. I became interested in telling the story of a people whose voices were left out of the historical record. So I went to graduate school to study early encounters in colonial America, and I finally finished that dissertation on Indian-European relations in 17ᵗʰ-century Albany. In 2006, after two years teaching in Pennsylvania, I got a job as an assistant professor of history at Le Moyne.

Then in February 2008, I became a crazy dog lady. I drove down to the Tompkins County SPCA on a bitterly cold day and left with Shelby, a one-year old, out-of-control, boxer/lab/Tasmanian devil mix who peed all over the floor at PetSmart, inhaled all her food, drooled incessantly, and immediately stole my heart and became the center of my world. She has more beds than I have rooms in the house; she has a collar and matching leash for every season. I enrolled her in weight-pulling competitions, and I even got her her very own custom-made, purple-and-yellow pulling harness with her name embroidered on both sides. I make sure she has an ample supply of cauliflower, her favorite snack. I am a proud crazy dog lady, and I am good at it.

At the time Shelby came into my life I was working on several research projects that came out of my dissertation dealing with American Indians, specifically Mohawks and Esopus, in the 17ᵗʰ century. This work was a continuation of my dissertation, and I had the goal of tenure in mind. I worked tenaciously at these projects, devoting holidays and weekends to revisions and rewrites, believing I was bringing a voice to an experience trapped in silence. Shelby would interrupt my work by dumping toys in my lap, a clear request to play, or by nudging my arm, a clear request to scratch her butt, or by going back and forth between me and the door, a clear request to go for a walk. How could I say no to the center of my world?

The articles were finally published, and I did receive tenure. I began a new project on Indians in Colonial cities, but at the same time a comment from an eminent historian who happened to be leading a seminar I attended years earlier kept running through my head. He said, "I really wanted to be a novelist, but I had nothing important to say, so I became an historian." I do not believe he saw his life's work as an historian unimportant. Uncovering the past is important, but what was the past I wanted to uncover? I was interested in Indian history because I saw myself as being able to give voice to a people whose voices had been silenced for centuries. However, historians of Native America have shattered that silence over the previous decades, particularly for the Iroquois, who, along with the Lakotas, are probably the most written about tribe in America.

More importantly, Native American historians began telling their own history. So, did I have anything to bring to that story anymore? I asked Shelby these questions as we took our daily walks or went on our marathon drives from Syracuse to Tennessee to visit family and back again. She would look at me intently, cock her head to the side, maybe lick my hand, maybe grab her leash to play, sometimes look away as if embarrassed at my incessant questioning, but she always remained silent. What is it that I really want to do? I want to uncover the stories and the experiences of those whose voices have been silenced in the historical record or who have had no voice at all.

Looking back through the historiography, or the history of the history, of America, one can see the evolution of the topics on which historians choose to write and the increasingly creative questions historians ask. Early Indian histories consisted of Europeans reading sources such as *The Jesuit Relations* and writing about the Indian barbarism, which they read in those pages. It was years before historians began asking different questions and actually asking Indians about their own histories. Historians have come a long way from Francis Parkman in the 19th century, who did not believe that Indians were or could be, civilized peoples, to the 21st century scholars such as Daniel Richter who wrote *Looking East from Indian Country*. Richter asked this simple question: If we look from west to east instead of following the path of the colonizers, how does that change current historical understanding of European colonization? This helped change the way students of history, his primary audience, understand the experiences and roles of Indian peoples as active participants in American history. We can be proud of the gains we've made.

Now historians such as Virginia DeJohn Anderson, who wrote *Creatures of Empire: How Domestic Animals Transformed Early America* (2004), are beginning to ask questions regarding the roles animals have played in the history of America. How had no one ever asked the question of how animals, particularly livestock, shaped the creation of a society based on agriculture and the idea that God had given humans dominion over those animals? Well, of course, for a long time, no one asked, "Hmmm, I wonder how Indian peoples understood those encounters with those Jesuits?" But once historians did, a whole new world was uncovered. Anderson's study concluded that the Euro-American empire in North America was built by humans, but that the active participation of non-human animal immigrants from Europe was also crucial to that experience: a pretty important role for dumb animals. Her work made me realize that there are more experiences that need to be uncovered. We just have to start asking some new questions and listen differently.

Now I find myself at the start of a new path, one with fewer human footprints but with many more paw and hoof prints. However, I keep the old path in sight and often find myself crossing over it, merging with it, and traveling down other paths I hadn't thought of. I am still grounded in my work in colonial American history and am using it to bring other characters, non-human animal characters, into the story, although writing of the experiences of animals is quite different from bringing voice to humans silenced in the record. Can we talk about animals as actors in history, or were they merely acted upon by humans? This new work has led me into environmental history, where scholars see the natural world as being both actor and acted upon; the environments in which we live and which we build shape our societies. Can we say the same for animals, or are non-human animals merely agents of human action? I believe that, in a world where we as a society argue about factory farming, overfishing, wolf hunts, buffalo preservation, and legal rights for animals, in a society where dogs have their own Facebook pages (Shelby does not have her own Facebook page, but she is the primary focus of mine) and are named as inheritors of mass fortunes, these are questions we should ask. It is worth knowing how we got to this point.

Starting over is a bit scary, but as with most events that frighten us, it also provides a bit of an adrenaline rush. I start from where I am—a crazy dog lady, an animal rights advocate, an aspiring vegetarian—and work to ask the right questions and to look at old sources with new eyes. I feel as if I should apologize to Shelby for not listening to her for all those years when she clearly was trying to answer my incessant questions about what I wanted to say and what I wanted to do and why I wanted to do it. I now understand why she turned away in embarrassment so many times. Luckily, a little cauliflower goes a long way toward forgiveness.

DAN ROCHE has published two memoirs—*Great Expectation: A Father's Diary* (Iowa, 2008) and *Love's Labors* (Riverhead, 1999)—plus essays in *Fourth Genre, River Teeth, The North American Review, Passages North, Stone Canoe,* and *Why We're Here: New York Essayists on Living Upstate* (Colgate, 2010). He was a 2005 Fellow in Nonfiction Literature with the New York Foundation for the Arts. He chairs the Communication & Film Studies Department at Le Moyne.

Beyondness

Dan Roche

My dad joined the Navy at seventeen, did eight years, got out and worked in the steel mills of Youngstown, Ohio, for four years, and then rejoined the military, this time the Air Force, in which he spent the next twenty-two years. Somewhere along the line, he took a literature class. He took classes over the course of much of his military career, mostly ones on management or techniques of warfare, but now and then some liberal arts ones. I assume they were required for the bachelor's degree toward which he was gradually working, and which he got when he was in his early fifties and I was in college myself.

In that lit class, he had to read a Hemingway story. It was one of the Nick Adams stories, which he referred to simply as "that Hemingway story," as if Hemingway had written only one. Or he called it "this story I had to read."

The story pissed him off for years. Decades. Well, let me be more exact. I don't think my dad had any issue with the story itself. What he groused about every time the subject came up was the way his teacher insisted he interpret the story.

The story takes place in Michigan's upper peninsula. I always thought that setting in itself would endear the story to my dad, because for eight years of my childhood he was stationed at Air Force bases in the UP, where he worked happily in the cold and snow taking care of B-52s. He had big, round, super-insulated boots and elbow-length mittens with leather palms and rabbit fur on the back and a thick, green hooded parka with his name in a blue stripe on the left chest. He liked the equipment of winter work. He and I used to take nighttime walks through the crunchy snow when it was fifteen below, and I would sometimes have to jog to keep up with his long strides. He would breathe in the frozen air deeply and proclaim how good the cold was. Stars hovered in the black sky. When I eventually read the Nick Adams stories—by which time I was living in the much less-invigorating landscape of southwestern Ohio—they filled me with nostalgia.

In the story, there is a forest fire. It's destructive and terrifying. My dad's teacher said that, sure, it was a forest fire in the upper peninsula of Michigan, but more importantly and interestingly, it was a metaphor for World War I. This interpretation did not sit well with my dad. What he said to me probably fifty or sixty times over the next thirty years was that the forest fire was a forest fire. Period. End of story. End of Hemingway. End of literary discussion.

Early on, I argued with him. Of course it was a metaphor, I said. I gave him some of my college-boy knowledge about Hemingway's time as an ambulance driver in war-torn Italy, about how he was seriously wounded, about how war was his Big Subject. Forget it, my dad said.

My dad's stubbornness surprised me partly because, for much of my childhood, he was the reader against whom I measured myself. He read fast and frequently. He liked history and thrillers. Leon Uris. Books about Ireland. He preferred the thick hardbacks, and he spent many, many hours lying on the couch with one of those books held open above his face. If it were a hot day, there might be a bottle of Coors on the floor next to him. It would usually take him only a day or two to finish a book. He'd stride through it as he strode through the cold Michigan nights.

And so, I never presumed—and still don't presume—that my dad wasn't a good reader, or that being able and willing to see metaphorical possibilities within a story might have been something he needed. He could see a metaphor when he wanted to. He just didn't search them out or appear moved by the ones that crossed his path. Besides, he'd done two tours in Vietnam—a direct experience with war which may very well have made him conclude that, for him if not for Hemingway, war wasn't something you implied by way of a more confined horror.

I admired metaphors right from the start, even in the sports biographies and crime books I favored during my early teen years. Joseph Wambaugh's *The Onion Field* attracted me as much by the question of what an onion field could symbolize as by the fact that the story told of a kidnapped Los Angeles police officer being shot to death in an actual onion field. I liked the mix of hard facts and figurative possibilities.

It took me a while to find a place where I could work with both.

At first, I went the route of solidity and job security: an undergrad major in mechanical engineering. I enjoyed the intellectual and pragmatic challenges offered by that profession, but the work left me mired in rigorous logic and hardnosed numbers, unable to imagine my way beyond the equations I sat at my desk solving. Though I was an adequate engineer, it became clearer each day I would never be a happy one. I missed words, thought about books, fixated enviously on that memory of my dad on the couch with the pages of a novel open above his face. I began taking night classes in writing and literature. During lunch hours and evenings, I read the stories of Flannery O'Connor, Russian novels, the poems of the Romantics. I discovered Keats' idea that the secret to achievement is the capability "of being in uncertainties, mysteries, doubts, without any irritable reaching after fact and reason." Reaching after fact and reason as an engineer, which was what I did all day, made me extremely irritable.

I left engineering as soon as I could swing it—for graduate school in English—but engineering didn't instantly leave me. My first literature paper was on the poetry of Wallace Stevens. The professor scribbled only this at the bottom: "You seem to think that art *must* provide answers." In her office the next day, she told me I might be happiest working in a library, where there were numbers and organized shelves.

I was convinced she'd misread me as badly as my dad was convinced his teacher had misread Hemingway.

I wanted to think more broadly, like a humanities major. How I'd learn that habit—especially since I was already in my mid-twenties—was unclear, though I began by throwing away all the pads of green graph paper I still had in stock, the kind on which I'd crunched so many numbers and circled so many definitive answers. I read *Zen and the Art of Motorcycle Maintenance* and saw, in Robert Pirsig's explanation of the differences between the classical mode of thinking and the romantic mode, my own fractured life. Where I'd been and where I wanted to go.

Many times, I let myself feel despondent about having taken the wrong path and wanted to erase engineering from my memory completely. But in calmer moments, I did not want the habit of scientific logic gone from my life. It served me well: mapping trips, building bookshelves. I only wanted it not to be everything, or even primary. I wanted to merge what I had and what I wanted more to be.

That merging did not come in an epiphany. The very atoms of my being did not one day align in perfect balance. Over the course of a decade or so, however, I made progress. I've made more progress in the two decades after that.

One early catalyst was that professor's pigeon-holing of me into a library job. Another came the very next term, in a nonfiction writing class that I signed up for not because I had any idea of what we'd do in there, but because the class would meet in a carpeted room furnished with a big circle of frumpy couches. The casualness of the room's interior design proved liberating, as it was probably meant to. In that class, I discovered a form that let me anchor myself in facts and roam widely in imagination, questions, and unknowingness.

That sounds big. It actually took me a while—well beyond the end of that term—to limber myself up as an essayist, to get a feel for how to make the roaming really wide. In that class, though, I had my first modest success. It came in a short and true narrative I wrote about an odd early morning in a small Ohio town while I was waiting for a Greyhound bus. I was strolling the streets, wasting time. An opossum, which had maybe also been wasting time, was hunched in the vestibule of a sporting-goods store. When the owner came to unlock his door, he and the opossum had a stand-off. Neither knew what to do. People came by on their ways to work. Some commented. Others jumped toward the street when they saw the animal. I tossed the opossum some peanuts I'd bought for the bus ride. For half an hour, there was this funny disruption to the start of a workday. Then a no-nonsense guy came along, thought we were all pansies, and scooted the opossum away from the door with his boot. I ended the essay with the opossum sauntering "alone down the street, slowly, not confidently, but as if it had just come out of a movie and was trying to reorient itself to the real world."

No answer, no moral. Just an image that enlarged the moment, if only slightly, beyond itself.

A rigorous study of music teaches you to think about the present and the future simultaneously. (You have to play the note you're on, while looking ahead to the measures coming.) I'd make a similar claim about writing essays with rigor: that it teaches you to think simultaneously about the tangible and the intangible.

That combination is my aim as an essayist—in the same way, I think, poets aim to go further than the words themselves. Such "beyondness" is not my only joy in essay-writing. There are more frequent pleasures in the crafting of sentences and paragraphs; in the searching through my favorite book—the *Oxford American Writer's Thesaurus*—for the exact and surprising word; in the cutting of phrases or passages that don't earn their ways into a final draft.

But it is the unforeseen and messy beyondness that interests me most as a writer. To put it in a way that might irk my dad: Metaphor (from the Greek *metaphorein*: to transfer, translate, carry over) is the essence of an essay.

I teach essay-writing as exploration, because I write essays myself as a way to explore. Explore what? I never know until I'm writing—usually along about the tenth or twelfth draft. Students don't generally do ten or twelve drafts, which is part of the reason that my encouragements for them to break out of the linear and the bounded are met with initial (even lingering) resistance and confusion.

For most of them, this is new territory. Their prior nonfiction writing has had to be formulaic and definitive: five-paragraph themes; argumentative essays; thesis and support; lab reports; or, as with my journalism students, facts, facts, and facts—with attributions. All necessary ways of writing, all appropriate to their times and places.

When we discuss any of their essays-in-progress, however, I always ask: "What is this about?" Their first-level answer is whatever's named: a high-school prom, Grandpa's cigar-smoking, a Michael Jackson song. Yes, I say, that's the nominal subject, the thing named. That has to be vivid and clear and developed. You have to tell that story really well. And then I ask: "What else is the essay *about?*" At those moments, I am like my dad's professor, wanting my students to imagine beyond the burned trees in order to see the Great War. Fairly often, they get pissed off.

And then they don't. That might take weeks, months. We'll do exercises to help. For example: *Write two paragraphs about an incredibly famous movie line. ("May the Force be with you." "You can't handle the truth!") But make your paragraphs about something besides the movie line. Start here, go there. Give yourself a subject that roots you, and a vision that lifts you.*

Eventually—slowly, and then often dramatically—they begin to see how everyday life can point beyond itself. They begin to experience their writing's potential for enlargement. They start to become essayists.

Beyondness in an essay—as in a poem or story—must be artistic and earned, and any leap should feel, to the reader, simultaneously surprising and inevitable. It's an elusive combination.

Nor do the leaps always happen, or need to.

Perhaps, for instance, there is a straight-line relationship between my dad's dismissal of a metaphoric reading of Hemingway's story and my decision to devote myself to the uncertainty and ambiguity of essay-writing. I could use my old logic to reach that conclusion. It's a fact that many times when I've been writing, I've been impelled into a broader questioning of my subject and my own experience simply by thinking of how my dad might stop at a certain point and say, "That's that."

Perhaps I write essays because my dad was the reader he was.

I could circle that answer and move on.

Or I could say that I don't much believe in straight-line relationships, that such explanations don't get at the many truths of a complicated story.

I'm sure, for instance, there is much I could investigate about why my dad's literalness with Hemingway still frustrates me, though it's been a decade or more since I heard him tell the same old story, and though he's been dead for three years. Perhaps I could imagine how his reading of Hemingway was just as valid as the professor's. Perhaps there are essays I need to write about how my dad and I diverged politically, religiously, socially.

If I take on that exploration, I'll start with the facts. I'll try to put on the page the tangible realities of him and of me and of us as father and son—the daily interactions, the conversations, the silences, the time I punched a hole in my bedroom door because I was infuriated with him, the times he stopped to let me catch up during those walks under the cold, black skies of northern Michigan. I'd want to recreate and dwell within all those immediacies, just as I'd hope that those tangibles would, somehow, lead me past themselves, if only a little bit, and that I'd be able, eventually, to discover what in this story is only itself and what could be—should be—more.

ANN RYAN is Professor of English and a Le Moyne alumna.
She is the editor of the *Mark Twain Annual,* and co-editor of
Cosmopolitan Twain (2008) and *A Due Voci: The Photography
of Rita Hammond* (2003). In 2013, she received the Henry Nash
Smith Award from the Center for Mark Twain Studies for lasting
contributions to the field. She is the 2014–17 O'Connell Chair of
the Humanities at the college.

What I Do, and Why I Do It at Le Moyne

Ann Ryan

I hadn't planned on becoming a professor, but I think that journey began thirty-three years ago, the day that I first set foot on the campus of Le Moyne College. I was a typical Le Moyne student at the time: the grand-daughter of Irish immigrants, the product of an average public school system, and the child of parents who wanted the best for me, despite their inability to finance those ambitions. I was sorely disappointed to be attending Le Moyne, an institution which both my sisters, and eventually my brother, would also claim as their alma mater. I wanted something more grand, something more exotic, a place with spires and marble and smart-looking co-eds who wore interesting scarves, a place where Kennedy stand-ins played touch football on "the quad," and pulled "all nighters" in medieval-looking libraries.

Clearly, I had been thumbing through the brochures available at the office of the guidance counselor; either that, or I had been watching *The Paper Chase, Love Story,* or possibly *The Way We Were.* To be honest, I wouldn't rule out *Animal House* as a source for my dreams about collegiate life. For me, college had all the allure of traveling abroad to some foreign land. And I had woven into my imaginings about college life all the romance and exoticism that I could glean from bad television and romantic movies.

Without quite realizing it, I had been casting myself in my own movie, full of location shots and sentimental dialogue. I wanted to be Ali MacGraw, the gorgeous co-ed from a working-class family; I wanted her long, silky brown hair and her Harvard boyfriend (played by Ryan O'Neill, before the metham-phetamine use and domestic assault charges). I wanted to walk, hand in hand, through some Ivy League campus with my fictional boyfriend—hair flowing behind me—and tell him that "love means never having to say you're sorry" (though even at eighteen I knew this was a really leaky definition of love).

Or I would have settled for being Barbra Streisand, the not-quite-as-gorgeous co-ed from a working-class family. She had wild, curly brown hair—not ideal—but as compensation she would eventually marry Hubble Gardner (played by Robert Redford, before the plastic surgery and simplistic liberalism). Like the strident Babs, I wanted to stand on the steps in front of some magnificent old building and make speeches about politics. (I wasn't actually that interested in politics, but my fictional self was.) And I fantasized that, someday, I would meet up with my "Hubble" in New York City (where I would live in fabulous brownstone with a newer, smarter, more appreciative husband), and tell him—as I glanced at the vapid WASP he was currently dating—that he had "a lovely girl" (both of us knowing, of course, that she'd never measure up to me).

Or, as a last resort, I wanted at least to belong to a sorority, to go to a wild toga party, wear sunglasses at night, and hang out with the cool kids. By day I wanted to sit in classrooms that looked old and serious and intense (*à la The Paper Chase*); at night, I wanted to go to some Animal House and drink beer with John Belushi, and dance with Tim Matheson, both to the music of Otis Day and the Nights.

In the end, all I got was the working-class family and the curly hair.

Le Moyne didn't look or feel the way I thought a college should: there were no spires, no marble statues, no frat houses, no mahogany-lined dining halls. When I walked on the campus of my dreams, I wanted a "love at first sight" feeling; I wanted some spectacular romance to begin. But when I toured Le Moyne it all felt familiar, friendly, somewhere between my high school—West Genesee—and my church—St. Michael's. I had spent a lot of time ornamenting my dreams of college life: filling them with the people I wanted to meet, costuming myself in new names and attitudes, narrating a life and scripting my role in it. But in none of my dreams, in none of the scenarios I had worked out for myself, did I envision riding a Centro bus to my first day of college classes, with a lunch packed by my mother; nor did I expect to return to my parents' home at the end of that first day.

I was a commuter student at Le Moyne College. It was the perfect marriage of humiliation and disappointment.

However—and surely there had to be a "however"—I soon found myself written into another kind of romance, one that I hadn't expected, and one that we never, ever make movies about. It's hard to describe, but I began to fall in love with thinking. And as it turns out, you don't need spires or mahogany or even a cute boyfriend to think well. I suppose the first change that I experienced at Le Moyne was this assault on the pre-packaged, formulaic narratives that I had been sold, and that I bought so readily. On film, in television, in the novels I read and the magazines I consumed up to that point, all my images of women were binary: ingénues vs. vixens; the pretty girlfriend vs. the lonely bookworm; the happy homemaker vs. the bitter working woman. None of it was thoughtful or nuanced; none of my Hollywood icons or romance-novel heroines was eccentric or original, political or funny, independent or self-determined. Of course, had I the impulse or the insight, I could have taken a look at my mother or my aunt, or any of the women in my neighborhood—most of whom didn't have professions and who would never find their lives reflected on any of the screens I worshipped. I would have found in them, and in their life stories, character worth emulating.

But I suppose that this is one of the wonderful consequences of a good education. Le Moyne didn't just take me to new places; it revealed to me the stories and histories that were all around me, from the green light on Tipperary Hill, to my grandmother's paystub from the Melvin Savings and Loan, to Father Kilpatrick's time in Vietnam, to the framed diploma my mother kept in a bottom drawer, to my father's childhood stories about helping my grandfather deliver milk on the West Side of Syracuse. What I learned at Le Moyne was to see beyond the surface of things, how to read more deeply into the world around me, and how to represent that world in ways that were authentic and compelling.

If it didn't look like the colleges in the pamphlets or those I saw in films, Le Moyne College soon felt like what I had longed for, what I needed without even knowing it. At Le Moyne we love to quote from *Walden* by Henry David Thoreau: "For a short time, I lived like a dolphin." It's always seemed to me the wrong passage, just as the dolphin always seemed an odd, disturbing choice for a mascot (who ever heard of a fighting dolphin?). If I'm going to look to *Walden* to represent my experience as a student at Le Moyne, I'd use Thoreau's paean to the morning: "The millions are awake enough for physical labor; but only one in a million is awake enough for effective intellectual exertion, only one in a hundred millions to a poetic or divine life. To be awake is to be alive." What I didn't realize at eighteen years old was that, while I thought of myself as a dreamer, I was actually just unconscious.

I think it's no exaggeration to say that the faculty of Le Moyne College woke me up. Granted, I was no Snow White (I was betting at the track at thirteen and knew how to tap a keg by the time I was fifteen). Still, at eighteen years old, I hovered somewhere between dead and asleep. This faculty awakened me to worlds of ideas, languages, histories, art, literatures, politics, and people, worlds of which I was wholly unaware. Looking back, it seems to me that my professors either brought me to life or they insisted upon bringing life to me; in any case, I grew out of my complacency, my silliness, and my self-absorption, and began to aspire to something higher, something more meaningful and engaged (and, who knows, maybe someday I'll make it to something "poetic or divine").

In my classes I heard words I had never heard before, in discussions that confused and excited me. They were woven into narratives that were original and complicated, with themes that didn't fit into any simple rendering of good and bad, right and wrong, male or female, us and them. My sense of place began to change. Le Moyne College ceased to be small, and local, and familiar; it became provocative, exciting, and worldly. The classroom at Le Moyne bridged the gap between the world that I had come from and the future I wanted to create for myself.

Thanks to Dr. Neil Novelli's course on Shakespeare, I saw my first performance of *Richard II* (in fact, my first performance of Shakespeare and my first experience of live theater of any sort). In Professor Rob Flower's introduction to philosophy class, I actually worried that my head would explode. I first heard the word "feminism" from Dr. Susan Bordo, who taught in both the Honors Program and in the Philosophy Department, and I learned about literary theory in a religious studies class led by Dr. Harry Nasuti. In Professor Pat Keane's freshman composition course, I learned that I didn't know how to write (shocking, since I had always been told that I was an *A* student), but that, with some effort, I had the potential to excel. And in Professor Rachel Romeo's Spanish class, we read the poetry of García Lorca and, for the first time, I spoke with a native speaker. (My high school Spanish teacher's name was Mrs. O'Brien.) Thanks to the efforts of Student Development, I went to my first museum, The Everson—then eventually to The Metropolitan and The National Portrait Gallery—traveled to Canada for the Stratford Festival, and went to New York City for my first time. While there, I ate something called a "bagel," which in 1981 was unheard of on the west side of Syracuse. At Le Moyne I had my first exposure to jazz, my first debate about the nature of faith, my first "B+," and then my first 4.0, my first time performing on a stage, my first discussion about race and ethnicity, and the list could go on and on. And while some of my experiences in college—most of what I thought was meaningful at the time—have receded into the dusky corners of my memory, what I learned and felt in the classroom has remained vibrant and sharp in my mind.

If you had told me back in 1981 that, excepting my years in graduate school, I would spend my life in Syracuse, and most of that time on the campus of Le Moyne College, I think I would have cried. I would have mourned the loss of the wider world, the glamorous life that I had dreamed of having. But what I've discovered now, in over twenty years as a college professor, is how vibrant and meaningful and, for lack of a better word, "big" this campus has been for me. I am a 19th-century Americanist, a Mark Twain scholar in particular; my work has centered on questions of race and identity; I teach classes about the literature of Harlem and the Wild West; I love to talk about the American Renaissance, and the work of Emerson, Thoreau, Alcott, Whitman, Dickinson, and Margaret Fuller. Each year I take students on trips, some quite local, to the summer home of Mark Twain in Elmira or to the Women's Rights National Park at Seneca Falls. Others are slightly more extensive; I regularly take students to Harlem, where we listen to jazz and tour museums; and occasionally I take them to Concord, Massachusetts, where we wander through the Sleepy Hollow Cemetery and walk around Walden Pond. I often team teach with colleagues at Le Moyne: Dr. Julie Grossman, who writes on American Film Noir and the Femme Fatale; or Dr. Julie Olin-Ammentorp, who specializes in the work of Edith Wharton; or Dr. Doug Egerton, an historian who publishes on American slavery and race in the 19th century.

Nothing excites me more than teaching: the dynamism, the unexpected flashes of insight from a student or a colleague. When I'm in the classroom, I feel as if I'm part of what Emerson called "the current of the universal being," by which he meant something that connects all of us, connects us through ideas, imagination, and inspiration. At those moments, Le Moyne doesn't seem small or familiar at all.

Of course, not everything has changed. I still live in Syracuse, still commute to campus, and I still bring my lunch with me to school.

MARY SPRINGSTON is Associate Clinical Professor and
Director of the Department of Physician Assistant Studies.
She earned her Master's at Le Moyne College and her PA
certificate from the Sophie Davis School of Biomedical Education
at Harlem Hospital. In 2011–12, she was awarded
the Global Outreach Humanitarian Award Grant from the
Physician Assistant Foundation, which allowed her to travel
to South Sudan to give workshops on HIV prevention.

Lessons Learned

Mary Springston

The long-awaited interview at the Harlem Physician Assistant program didn't go quite the way I had anticipated. On that fateful morning in 1990, I got off the subway in Harlem at 137th Street and Malcolm X Boulevard. I followed the instructions that I had excitedly written when I was offered the interview, briskly walking past Harlem Hospital, being sure to stay on the south side of the street to avoid the crack houses as I had been instructed, stepping over cigarette butts and trash, and holding my breath as I passed an area that smelled of urine. After what seemed like an eternity, I finally arrived at the building that housed the Physician Assistant Program on the fifth floor. The old elevator creaked and moaned as it brought me up to the department that I had dreamed about; my future was on the other side of the door. "What an opportunity!" I said to myself as I thought how this still-young and unique profession might allow me to care for other human beings, body and soul. All that I knew up until this point in my life, and all that I had read about regarding this exciting field, compelled me to pursue it with more vigor than I'd brought to anything I had ever done before. There I was; this was my moment. I arrived in a room full of equally hopeful, vigorous and motivated applicants who all wanted the same thing I did: an opportunity to change the course of their lives forever.

I was called to my first interview by a very stern-looking black woman who immediately appeared to be put off by me for some reason. I had no idea why this was happening, as I had not even spoken a word yet, but the tension in the room was undeniable. Her first question: "What are *you* going to do for *this* community?" Despite her tone and attitude, her inquiry was stirring, and I found myself looking deeply into my heart. What *was* I going to do for this community—or any other community I might want to serve later in my potential career? Had I even thought that far ahead? The fact that I was white compounded the difficulties that day, and would continue to do so in the long days ahead.

I waited anxiously in the weeks that followed to hear about my interview status, only to discover that I wasn't accepted into the program. Many months later, after the initial disappointment was finally becoming less painful, I received a call one morning saying that the school had received grant money and could now take two more students; however, I would have to start tomorrow because the program classes had already begun one week earlier! I made my decision immediately; I gave notice to the research lab where I was working and would continue to finish my experiments on weekends, and started on a transformative educational experience and life journey.

I learned many valuable lessons in PA school; many of those lessons had nothing to do with the science of medicine, but still serve me well today. Our program director was a no-nonsense, burly man, often found with a pipe in his mouth. Upon our first meeting with him, he said to us, "Nothing in life is fair." In retrospect, I'm certain this was his way of preempting complaints regarding the long study hours and arduous lifestyle we would be encountering. He went on to say that unless we were referring to a fair with a Ferris wheel, or a token for the subway, we were not to use the word "fair." The director was one of the nation's first PAs and would frequently regale us with fascinating stories about the origin of our profession. Listening to him while integrating my own youthful experiences in the career, I came to discover the injustices of a broken healthcare system. Once I saw this firsthand, I took his advice to heart and deleted the word "fair" from my vocabulary.

The first year of PA school was incredibly challenging: I worked hard, then harder, then harder still. My sustenance was in knowing that everything I was trying to learn would help someone someday. I often wondered if were possible to put even one more tiny fact into my brain, but before I knew it, I had successfully completed the academic rigors of the first year and had set sail for my second year, which would consist of clinical rotations.

On my first day of surgery, I arrived to learn that a patient had just jumped out of a window after he woke up in the ICU and discovered that he had failed in an earlier attempt to commit suicide. This time, he landed on a recently installed hyperbaric chamber that was three stories below, and for the second time in his life, his effort to end it was thwarted. I was directed to bring him to radiology for a CT scan. I can still hear him screaming to let him go to the bathroom, knowing very well that he would make another attempt on his life if I caved in to his pleas.

I was reminded of my program director's words to always consider the entire patient, physically and mentally. This rather novel approach to healthcare, which later became known as the biopsychosocial spiritual paradigm of medicine, became the cornerstone for me as I continued to diagnose patients during my training and develop my own personal style of medical practice. I learned how to really listen and always look. I recall an incident that occurred in an over-crowded inner-city emergency room. The ER had two areas to treat patients: one section handled the surgical patients, and the other, the medical ones. One day, the overworked and underpaid nurse was pleading with me to quickly address an issue of urinary retention in an elderly male who kept complaining about leg pain and a swollen ankle. I was told multiple times to hurry up so that the patient could be moved out of the surgical area of the ER to the medical section. I attempted to focus my questions only on the retention issue, but the elderly man kept talking about his leg. As soon as the nurse left the room, I decided to do a quick course change of my physical exam and asked the patient if I could take a look at his leg. I was utterly shocked when I was finally able to see it. Essentially, nothing was left except for dry, dark skin that was firmly attached to his bones. My determined listening had paid off, and I was able to get the patient admitted to the surgical unit, where he was able to get the care he needed.

On occasion during those years, a few patients—and sometimes staff— would remind me that I "didn't belong" in Harlem. One such patient, racked with late-stage illness, literally crawled after me in order to shout, "White bitch, go home!" The noble life of giving that I had imagined fractured rather quickly, like a face mirror dropped unexpectedly on a ceramic floor. The shards of my new career were painful sometimes, and I quickly learned that not everyone was going to tolerate my presence, or accept my good intentions and hard work. Fewer still would say, "Thank you." That's just the way it was.

I think at that point in my life I decided to make an even more concerted effort to work specifically with people in desperate need of healthcare in order to prove to them that my intentions were selfless and that I had no hidden agenda. Easier said than done. In time, however, most came to realize that I was not going to abandon my seriously ill patients in these underserved communities. Day after day, I gave my best effort and moved forward at a slow but steady pace. I kept in mind that my purpose was one of service and altruism. People began to take notice, and before I knew it, I was a part of the community, even if peripherally so.

I could see my experiences build upon each other, as layer by layer, my own mission revealed itself to me; I did not have to seek it. Mine was to address healthcare disparities in areas typically shunned by my own colleagues. The process of acceptance is a long one and goes both ways. Each day was tough, but as the days followed one another, I became clearer and clearer about my career path. In that phase of my life, I could never have dreamed that I would eventually be invited to teach future PAs in these same communities, or that the experience of sharing knowledge with the next generation would be so powerful for me.

It was shortly after this time that I found myself working on Riker's Island with an incarcerated HIV/AIDS patient population. The random clinical rotation assignment turned out to be a pivotal point in my career. The many patients I cared for prepared me to work later with people living with HIV at Bellevue Hospital following my hard-earned graduation. I believe that when one works in medicine—particularly in underserved, impoverished areas characterized by a sense of despair and hopelessness, or in the fields of oncology or HIV/AIDS with seriously, medically ill patients—one finds God in all places and things. Long before I knew the Jesuit concept of *magis*, I understood that doing more for others was simply part of my DNA.

During the early years of the HIV epidemic, care for people who were HIV-positive or who had AIDS was primarily focused on healing efforts, controlling opportunistic infections, improving the quality of one's remaining life, bringing closure and resolution to various issues, and striving for a peaceful death with dignity. But by 1996, the advent of the protease inhibitor medications allowed patients to live longer, healthier lives. Many of my patients had already developed short-term goals, such as hoping to live long enough to see a son turn sixteen, or to see a grandchild born. But now, they could look a bit further into their future.

I recall working with one woman who had to bring her young boy with her to our clinic. My patient couldn't afford a babysitter, so her ten-year-old son arrived in tow with her. The clinic was strategically placed in a corner of the hospital with a discreet sign reading "Virology." However, an illness by any other name is still that illness, and most people who knew us came to refer to our "Virology" clinic as what it actually was: the "HIV Clinic." At that time, there was still a lot of stigma associated with HIV, and confidentiality laws were still being developed and evolving in order to protect patients from experiencing the discrimination that was so rampant during those days. Our corridor was avoided by anyone who could find another corridor to walk down instead.

My patient's son sat quietly in the corner of the room as I spoke to his mother about her antiviral medications. The treatment was working perfectly; her viral load was at its target level of "undetectable." Yet, she wanted to go off the medications because of horrible side effects she was encountering called liposdystrophy. This redistribution of body fat made her look fat and disfigured. The medicine had given her a triple chin and a large mound of fat where her neck met her upper back (referred to as a "buffalo hump"). In spite of my best educational efforts and support, it was clear that my attempt to convince her to remain on this life-saving medication regimen was for naught. As I was losing my argument inch by inch, her quiet son suddenly spoke up and said, "Mommy, you look beautiful to me!"

As the years passed, I elected to move to upstate New York. I interviewed with Le Moyne College when the opportunity presented itself, and I'm glad to say that that interview went much better than my initial interview at the Harlem PA program. The concept of an academic culture made me somewhat uncomfortable at first, as I had become so used to practicing medicine in underserved communities during the previous decade. However, my strength was derived from my passion for teaching as a result of having been an adjunct professor for many years in the Bronx and Harlem. I had on many occasions already felt the energy that surges forth when learning is taking place and individuals are engaged and sharing knowledge for the greater good.

At the Le Moyne interview, the dean kindly handed me the college's mission statement. As I read it, I recognized that the words were a reflection of the life I had already been living. In that instant, I understood that the opportunity to teach at a Jesuit institution, to embrace the biopsychosocial spiritual paradigm of medicine, was something that I not only endorsed fully, but had been doing all of my professional life. The opportunity to provide a transformative educational experience to the next generation of PA students fulfilled my life ambitions in the most positive way. The concept of *cura personalis* was already known to me, though the Latin phraseology was new. Caring for the "whole patient" was something I had done from day one. My ability to be compassionate, that is "to suffer with" my patients, was something I had learned a long time ago. Coming to Le Moyne was coming home, full circle.

I continued to practice medicine after accepting my appointment at the college. Every Thursday afternoon I would volunteer at a local correctional facility, and work with people who were HIV-positive or who had AIDS. This was a calling I took on wholeheartedly, and it complemented my educational endeavors in the classroom. I believe we are all lifelong learners, and even though I had practiced medicine for quite some time, there was one Thursday afternoon that I remember well. The prison nurse told me she had an "extra-challenging patient" for me. The patient rolled into my examination room in his wheelchair as I was reading his extremely complicated medical history. That history included multiple spinal cord surgeries, which was the reason the staff had provided him with the wheelchair in the first place. Remembering my original lessons in learning how to listen carefully, I took the time to speak to him and get to know him better, rather than just focusing solely on his chief complaint. The patient told me about his concerns regarding his dog. He worried about who would care for the dog while he was incarcerated, and since I am a dog lover myself, we shared a few dog stories at that point. He calmed down very readily and began to engage me in a more thoughtful conversation. We agreed that his neighbor would be a good surrogate dog-daddy until my patient was released. He was okay with that. It occurred to me at this point in the conversation that it must have been very difficult for him to walk his dog regularly prior to being incarcerated. So I asked him how he managed to do that in a wheelchair. "I just walk the dog myself, because I can walk!" he said nonchalantly. It was at that moment that I discovered that my patient wasn't paralyzed at all! He could most certainly walk and had been doing so before being arrested. No one had taken the time to talk to him or listen to what he was saying. To prove my point, I had him walk over to the scale in the room to be weighed. I admit I had a smile on my face imagining how the nurses would react when I told them I had performed a miracle and that this man no longer would need a wheelchair while in prison!

As I look over my career to date, I am often struck by the ripple effect that my educational training has had on me, both as a healthcare provider and an educator. Medical facts hold little meaning unless one applies these concepts to the entire person compassionately. When one looks at the whole picture, and not just a small piece of it, one can better understand the patients' needs, improve the quality of their lives and strengthen their support systems. Now a program director myself, I practice *cura personalis* with my own students; I care for them the way I want them to care for their patients.

With each successive generation, medicine and psychiatry advance in great leaps and bounds. Yet still at the core of our practice remains the human heart. The incorporation of competence with compassion is the cornerstone of my program and my personal belief system. I hope that through our faculty role-modeling, we are able to prepare the next generation of PA healthcare providers with the best opportunity to go out into the world and really make a difference. I urge them all to do well, but more importantly to do good.

MILES TAYLOR has taught literature and writing courses at
Le Moyne since 2003. A Seattle native, he completed his Ph.D. on
renaissance drama at the University of Oregon. His scholarship on
Jacobean and Caroline theatre has been published in a variety of
journals. He and his wife, Erin (a medievalist by trade), have three
boys, two dogs, and a cat, and are thus vastly outnumbered.

A Person Made
Out of Words

Miles Taylor

Sylvia Plath once wrote a poem called "Cut" about accidentally slicing open her thumb in the kitchen. It begins, "What a thrill! My thumb, instead of an onion," and then goes on to make metaphor after metaphor out of her wound. ("Out of the gap a million redcoats run, traitors everyone," she writes, so that her blood cells become British soldiers treacherously fleeing the battle). But go back to that word "thrill." The earliest meaning of "thrill" is a hole, so that the hole in your nose is the nose-thrill, or nostril. To thrill something is to pierce it with a weapon, as Plath pierces her thumb. But we probably think first of the more common sense, "a slight shudder or tingling through the body; a penetrating influx of feeling or emotion." And that's just where the poem starts, with that thrill. It moves from that sharp shock of emotion and becomes art by building one image upon another upon another.

I get a thrill out of words. I am moved by them and pierced by them. I am enlightened by the stories they tell us about the past and about where we are now. Some words seem debased or depreciated, and that teaches me about where we are in relation to where we've been. Other words seem young and vital, even words a thousand years old. And when a great writer arranges these remarkable signs in ways that amaze and amuse, that harrow and haunt, I want to be there. Why? Because I believe our experience is (almost) always mediated by language, and so the more we fall in love with words and want to know more about them—love is always a hunger for knowledge about the object of our love—the more we are able to experience of life. But beyond that, to read a Shakespeare or an Austen or a Chaucer or a Plath is to be intimately in the presence of another person who through words becomes alive to us in ways we are hardly even alive to ourselves.

When I get beyond seeing words as everyday objects, as mundane things, there are infinite riches to be mined. There are treasures in finding a new word, and there are treasures in discovering in an old one some meaning or nuance or trace of a history I had not known. And those riches are every-where if we look for them. I'm typing on a keyboard, for example, and just above and to the right of my right pinky are a couple of keys with brackets on them. The typographical sense of the word *bracket* entered the English language in the mid-18th century, but two centuries earlier, when it first entered the language in the 16th century, the word *bracket* signified a piece of stone or wood jutting from a wall on which a statue could be placed. In the 17th century, it took on a new meaning, becoming a term in carpentry for the support created at the juncture of two pieces of wood or metal joined at a right angle. Now go back and look at the bracket on the keyboard, and you see it. It's a vertical structure with two perpendicular lines running from it. Like ornamental shelves, or like the braces used to join wood in carpentry. And it didn't stop changing there. We have income brackets, for example, entering the language in the Victorian era.

But where had the word *bracket* traveled before it entered English? As Mark Forsyth relates in his marvelous book *The Etymologicon*, *bracket* comes from Latin *braca* via French *braguette* or Spanish *bragueta* and was originally the singular of the Latin word meaning breeches. A breech was a "garment covering the loins and thighs." Linguists have suggested "the 'bracket' of architecture may have been so called from its resemblance to the 'codpiece' of a pair of breeches (Sp. *bragueta* meant both 'codpiece' and 'bracket')." Think about that for a minute. Someone looked at a piece of wood sticking out from a wall and thought it looked like a codpiece. If you've never seen a medieval codpiece, you would be surprised at how much it emphasized the wearer's endowment. Those brackets on your keyboard originally started life as the ornamental, exaggerated decorative leather pouches by which men displayed their manhoods.

Now what if someone wears his *bragueta*/codpiece and struts about? It's a form of vaunting, of boasting, of swaggering or showing off. And there I'm relating the *Oxford English Dictionary*'s definition of *brag*, because the word *bragging* is related to brackets. If you wear a particularly exaggerated bracket, you're a braggart.

What this word history, or etymology, tells us is that someone once saw an ornamental shelf sticking out from a wall and thought it looked like an exaggerated phallic display, and that's how the shelf took its name. And that was a metaphor. Generations later, someone thought that the right angles where carpenters joined materials looked like those shelves, and so they were called by that name. And that was a metaphor. And a hundred years later, the squared-off punctuation marks that set apart text looked like those carpenters' angles (and perhaps too, spatially or metaphorically, the text added in brackets seemed to be tacked on in the perpendicular, so to speak), so they were called by that name, and that was a metaphor. Still later, a Victorian bishop thought the socioeconomic strata were so rigid that he borrowed the name of the punctuation mark to designate the separation of classes. And that, too, was a metaphor. An economic class is a punctuation mark is a carpenter's juncture is a shelf is a codpiece. A metaphor of a metaphor of a metaphor of a metaphor.

Language works that way. Words move through time, picking up new figurative meanings that later become literal, losing old literal meanings (but maybe always maintaining traces of those early senses), forking off and becoming two new branches of words, and splitting again.

Taken just as objects themselves, words are fascinating.

But we're even luckier than that, because we have great poets and playwrights and writers of fiction who love the language, who have a mastery over it that astonishes us, who turn words in new ways, and who use language as the instrument through which they produce beautiful art.

I can hardly look at the bracket on my keyboard without smiling, without imagining some strutting medieval prince with a comically embellished codpiece. When I turn to literature, the riches there seem infinite. Hamlet dying charges Horatio to tell his story, and the name Horatio is a play on the word oration. Likewise, the would-be conqueror who takes the crown of Denmark when its royal family is extinguished is named Fortinbras, which means strong arm. Both men at the end of the play come to embody the names they've always carried. They are persons made out of words, as are, of course, all characters in Shakespeare and, for us, Shakespeare himself. And I, too—I am a person made out of words.

Someone who studies the English renaissance, as I myself do, once wrote of his career that he began with the desire to speak with the dead. And that is just what words allow us, and what great literature offers us—a chance to get outside of our own immediate present.

If I were locked in an eternal present tense, I would be a prisoner. There would be no way to imagine how things could be different, or better, or indeed much worse. Our language and our literature put us in dialogue with the dead, and the dead have a lot to say. They teach us that love is not love that alters when it alteration finds. They show us that just because the pardoner on his way to Canterbury is not a good man, he can still tell a good tale and save others' souls, even as he loses his own. We know that a young man of great fortune must be in want of a wife, or at least that that's what we'd need to believe if we were poor and had five daughters to dispose of in marriage. I am a student of life, and the language and literature I study are the best teachers I have known.

ROBERT THURBER is a documentary filmmaker whose work has
been screened at major film festivals in the United States and
Europe, as well as at the Museum of Modern Art in New York.
Several of his documentaries have been broadcast on
PBS, including the series *Frontline*. He holds an M.F.A in
filmmaking from New York University and an M.F.A. in theater
from Catholic University.

Why I Love
Making Documentaries

Robert Thurber

T he first shot I made that I couldn't cut or even trim in the editing room was of Roy Edmonds, a young prizefighter who had just turned pro. He was working on the heavy bag in Gleason's Gym, a ratty old loft on the south side of Union Square in Manhattan. It was a hand-held shot with a wide-angle prime lens—no zoom, because in those days the optical qualities of a zoom could never match the sharp yet subtle tones rendered by a prime—and Roy was pounding the bag, making it swing in a different direction with each blow. He would circle left or right depending on which way the bag was coming back at him, and would hit it high or low with his left or right, or sometimes with a rapid combination of blows. Working with the heavy bag is a drill—pounding, timing, and foot-work is what it's all about.

I moved in with my camera on my shoulder and with my right eye looking through the viewfinder composing the shot—keeping Roy and the bag in some sort of balance within the frame—while my left eye was open wide trying to take in my surroundings in a peripheral sort of way. Mainly I didn't want to walk into a punch that I didn't see coming, but also I needed a rough idea of what was going on around me—where I was in relationship to Roy and the bag, and what might be his next sequence of moves.

The shot lasted three minutes—the length of a round of boxing—and as I got the rhythm of the movement, I could feel myself moving in close and then stepping back when the shot needed to breathe. It became one of those things where your mind isn't working, but your body is. I had the sense of understanding something at the same time that I was learning it, and it was all happening in the part of my nervous system that was below my neck.

I got in behind Roy, right over his shoulder as he pounded the bag in a series of rapid combinations. I stepped back as he circled to the left and the bag swung in my direction from the right. I got behind the bag and could see into

Roy's eyes as he made his next move. His face squeezed as he pounded the bag with enough force to lift it a few inches. It snapped back down with a couple of clinking sounds from the chain that held it bolted to the ceiling. Roy slid again to his left, and I moved right—passing behind the back of the bag to face him on the other side, where he did the same thing again, using all his strength and power to punish the bag.

The shot goes on. The image moves with Roy and the bag—sometimes in close so that you feel like you are seeing what he sees and knowing what he knows; and sometimes the image pulls back for a wider view and a bit of a breather, simply watching Roy move with the sway of the bag. It was one of the best shots I've ever done, like a dance—the boxer, the bag, and the camera—choreographed intuitively inside a small circle and without any mistakes.

When I first saw the rushes they were on a big screen and everyone just went, "Oooo" and "Ahhhh." Camera-people love this kind of stuff and usually are willing to fight to the death to keep their best work in a film exactly as they shot it because editors are known to be ruthless cutting out what they decide needs to go. Since I was both the cameraman and the editor for this film, I knew what needed to be done. That responsibility meant that I had to give myself extra time to consider how the shot should play in the film—how it should be experienced—because it had to be more than the cameraman's vanity shot—lots of ego but not much purpose beyond showing off. The images were already there, so I turned my attention to the sound track because a carefully constructed track focuses the viewer's imagination on things that can't be seen. I worked with a great sound guy in the gym, and he had picked up the punches hitting the bag, Roy's breathing and grunting, and the chain snapping back after he lifted the bag into the air. He also had another track of ambient sounds from the gym itself. I mixed and adjusted the sound levels to bring the viewer deeper into the world inscribed by the bag and the boxer. Sometimes I boosted the audio of Roy's breathing and the blows to the bag; sometimes I brought in more background audio when it felt like we needed a little more space around the bag; and, when the camera went in close on Roy's face I lowered the audio so that the scene was almost silent, allowing his eyes do all the work.

My intention throughout the shooting and editing of any documentary is to transport the viewer's imagination to a place it never expected to be, to meet people he or she never expected to know, and to come away with an insight into human experience that had never before been considered. "The Boxer" is only twenty-five minutes long and even though it took me about a month to shoot and three months to edit, those twenty-five minutes are a carefully constructed distillation of not only what I saw and heard, but also what I thought, wondered, and learned to be true. To move with Roy around the heavy bag allowed us to cross briefly into a territory of his world and bear silent witness to the discipline, the will, and the grace with which he pursued a dream. I've carried that moment with me ever since.

ABOUT OUR EDITORS

Ned Stuckey-French (EDITOR) is the author of *The American Essay in the American Century* (Missouri, 2011), which was a *Choice* Outstanding Academic Book for 2012. He is also co-editor of *Essayists on the Essay: Montaigne to Our Time* (Iowa, 2012), co-author of *Writing Fiction: A Guide to Narrative Craft* (Longman, 9th ed.), book review editor of *Fourth Genre,* and an associate professor of English at Florida State University. He has also taught as an adjunct professor in the M.F.A. program at Columbia University. His articles and essays have appeared in journals such as *In These Times, The Missouri Review, The Iowa Review, The Normal School, Tri-Quarterly, Walking Magazine, culturefront, Pinch, Guernica, middlebrow,* and *American Literature,* and been listed five times among the notable essays of the year in *Best American Essays.*

Julie M. Elman (LAYOUT AND DESIGN) is an associate professor in the School of Visual Communication at Ohio University in Athens, where she teaches courses in publication design. She has more than 15 years industry experience in newspaper design and photojournalism. She designed *The New York Times* best-selling photography book *The Rise of Barack Obama* by Pete Souza, the chief White House photographer, and co-authored *The Newspaper Designer's Handbook* (7th ed.). She received her M.F.A. in photography from Ohio University and a B.F.A. in commercial art from the University of Dayton.

Michelle Grasek (COPY EDITOR) graduated from Le Moyne in 2007 with a major in Biology and a minor in English literature. She is an acupuncturist, treats patients at Monroe Community Hospital in Rochester, and works at the Finger Lakes School of Acupuncture & Oriental Medicine in Seneca Falls. She learned to love writing creative nonfiction at Le Moyne and is thrilled to enter the world of editing.